THE REMNANTS

ESSAYS, INTERVIEWS & OTHER WRITINGS

ZOLTAN ISTVAN

Copyright (c) 2021 Rudi Ventures LLC
(otherwise, all permissions granted for use)
Published by Rudi Ventures LLC
Cover Design: Rachel Edler
ISBN#: 978-1-7363426-5-7

****

AUTHOR'S NOTE

While these essays and writings have been arranged and edited for readability, many of them appear similar (if they are not new) to how they were originally published. Attempts have been made to preserve the context and moment in time they were written. Some articles contain British spelling. Publishing information and fact checks can be found by utilizing the Appendix.

****

TABLE OF CONTENTS

INTRODUCTION

CHAPTERS

I: Initial Musings

1) A Chip in my Hand Unlocks my House. Why Does that Scare People?

2) The New Bionic Sports of the Future Transhumanist Olympics

3) #TalktoMe: Futurist Zoltan Istvan Interviews his Aging Father

4) Cybernetics: More Transhuman than Human; Rumination on Cybernetic Technology

5) A TEDx Talk Celebrating Scientists and Exploring the Technological Future of Beauty

6) Will Brain Wave Technology Eliminate the Need for a Second Language?

7) *Quartz*: We Asked Some of the Boldest Thinkers What the World will be like in 50 Years. Here's what Zoltan Istvan Told Us

II: Diving Deeper

8) The 5 Most Revolutionary Scientific Trends to Look Out For (2017)

9) The First International Beauty Contest Judged by Robots

10) Major Transhumanism Conference Features Both Rising and Seasoned Experts

11) Is College Worth It? What Would You Have Paid to Get Your Degree?

12) The Augmented Expo in San Jose was Fascinating

13) Think Driverless Cars Will be Modern-looking and Reduce Traffic. Think Again

14) I Tried Direct Neurofeedback and the Results Surprised Me

III: Politics

15) A Transhumanist Goes to the Presidential Conventions

16) The Libertarian Futurist's Case for Avoiding War and Military Entanglements

17) Is Monetizing Federal Land the Way to Pay for Basic Income?

18) Why I'm Not Taking Any Contributions for my Presidential Run

19) To Grow 3rd Party Politics in America, Make John McAfee the Libertarian Party Nominee (Updated Version)

20) Gary Johnson Wants Driverless Secret Service Cars and a US-Led Gene Editing Revolution

21) I Went to the Largest Freedom Festival in the World and Here's What I Saw

22) Another Wild Week in my Transhumanism Campaign

23) I Want My Felonies Back

24) Should We Also Have A Small Private Market for the Coronavirus Vaccine?

IV: The *Psychology Today* Interviews Conducted by Zoltan Istvan

25) Wanted: A New Psychology; Interview with Futurist Gray Scott

26) Transhumanist Nikola Danaylov Faces Tragedy with Resolve

27) Gennady Stolyarov: A Children's Book Ponders Death

28) Interview with Transhumanism Advocate Riva-Melissa Tez

29) Interview with Transhumanist Activist Hank Pellissier

30) Exploring a New Type of Community: Zero State

31) Women in STEM, Transhumanism, and a New Author to Watch

32) TransEvolution, Transhumanism, and Daniel Estulin

33) Interview with Transhumanist Biohacker Rich Lee

34) Author David Simpson Talks Transhumanism in Science Fiction

35) *Longevity Cookbook* is Your Chance to Defeat Aging: Interview with Maria Konovalenko

36) Dr. Bertalan Mesko: A Medical Futurist Discusses Health and Transhumanism

V: Early Journalism

37) Discovering a Bush Tribe in the South Pacific

38) Does Landmark Unmanned Flight Spell Doom for Test Pilots?

39) For the Athens 2004 Olympic Games, Environmental Stakes are High

40) The World Under Sail

41) Travel! Intrigue! Cannibals! Extreme Journalism at Far Ends of Earth

42) Becoming a Treasure Hunter

43) The X Factor: My Pirate Attack off Yemen

44) Greening the Iron Curtain

45) The Mondavi of Pot

VI: A Collage of Work

46) Sad News: My Dad Steven Gyurko has Died

47) A Twitter Conversation Between Harvard University Center for Bioethics Faculty Member Dr. Louise Perkins King and Transhumanist Zoltan Istvan

48) I Almost Died from a Leading American Killer: Choking on Food

49) Interview with my Mom, Ilona Gyurko

50) Quotes and Reactions from my Wife, Dr. Lisa Memmel

51) Poem: *Death*

52) Song: *The Anti-You*

53) Cato Institute's *Cato Unbound* Debate: A Rebuttal: Deniers and Critics of AI Will Only Be Left Behind

54) Remarks on my Novel *The Transhumanist Wager*

55) Stop Impersonating me on Senior Dating Sites, Donating Fake Twitter Followers to My Presidential Campaign, and Vandalizing my Wikipedia Page

56) On Culture's Humanicide

57) A Bond with Hungary

58) Feature Documentary *IMMORTALITY OR BUST* Press Release

59) Foreword for Chris T. Armstrong's Book *At Any Cost: A Guide to the Transhumanist Wager and the Ideas of Zoltan Istvan*

VII: Commissioned XPRIZE Screenplay

60) XPRIZE Longevity Screenplay: *Humanity's Greatest Quest*

APPENDIX

AUTHOR'S BIOGRAPHY

ABOUT THE BOOK

******

INTRODUCTION

The Remnants: Essays, Interviews, & Other Writings is the seventh and final book of the box set collection of my futurist writings. The six books before this one are individually curated around the topics of transhumanism, futurism, life extension, secularism, politics, and philosophy. *The Remnants* is all the essential work that didn't make it into those books—but don't for a moment think of these writings below as leftovers. I think many readers and supporters of my work will find *The Remnants* the most interesting of the box set, as especially the later chapters contain many unusual parts of my writing history: including a poem on death; a sacrilegious song from my band days when I was a guitarist; a sampling of my humanitarian/science journalism before my public transhumanist career; a Twitter debate with Harvard University's Bioethics Department; my screenplay for an animated XPRIZE video; a public eulogy for my father; discussions with family members; and other more personal pieces.

The book also contains many interviews I made of people who I believe are interesting in the transhumanism movement. There's also commentary on my novel *The Transhumanist Wager,* as well as documents relating to feature documentary IMMORTALITY OR BUST and Chris T. Armstrong's book, *At Any Cost: A Guide to The Transhumanist Wager and the Ideas of Zoltan Istvan.*

Finally, this book also contains the largest amount of unpublished work of my futurist box set, including essays deemed too controversial or unorthodox for release in my usual media outlets.

I consider my box set, the *Zoltan Istvan Futurist Collection*, to be an essential highlight of my transhumanism career. And below in *The Remnants* are some of those final essays and reflections that helped complete that collection of work.

Zoltan Istvan / December 8, 2021

CHAPTER I: INITIAL MUSINGS

1) A Chip in my Hand Unlocks my House. Why Does that Scare People?

Over the past few decades, microchip implant technology has moved from science fiction to reality; today hundreds of thousands of people around the world have chips or electronic transmitters inside them. Most are for medical reasons, like cochlear implants to help the deaf hear. More recently, body-modification enthusiasts and technophiles have been installing microchips in their bodies that do everything from start a car to send a text message to make a payment in bitcoin.

The market for nonmedical implant technology is virtually unregulated, despite the fact that thousands of people around the world got chipped in the past 12 months. That may be about to change: Over the past few years, calls to heavily regulate or even ban voluntary implants have grown increasingly loud. There's a place for regulating implants, like any technology — but also a need to separate the fear from the reality.

I was excited to get my implant in 2015 at a biohacker gathering called Grindfest in Tehachapi, Calif. — specifically, in a garage in a dentist's chair, surrounded by vintage medical posters. These implants — often called radio-frequency ID or near-field-communication tags, depending on the technology involved — are about the size of a grain of rice and are installed in people in seconds via an oversize syringe. They each have a unique identification number and cost as little as $50. Most people get them injected in the tissue between their thumb and index finger.

Microchipping is still a fun part of a semi-underground culture, but interest is growing in more serious quarters. In 2016, the

Navy asked me to consult on a study led by James P. Wisecup, a retired vice admiral and the director of the Chief of Naval Operations Strategic Studies Group. One of the concerns they had was how civilian implants in sailors could affect the workings of a nuclear submarine.

More recently, implanting made national news when a Wisconsin technology company called Three Square Market announced it was having a chipping party for its employees. Workers were offered implants that allowed them to be tracked at work, replacing timecards. Workers could also use the implants to operate copy machines and buy food from the company's vending machines.

Not surprisingly, such interest from the military and the corporate sector has raised concerns, and not just among civil libertarians. Religious advocates have cautioned against the ethical challenges of implants. In February, Skip Daly, a Democrat in the Nevada State Assembly, introduced a bill to make involuntary microchip implants illegal; he later amended it to include voluntary microchipping as well.

The bill — even though it is in just one state and has yet to pass — set off a storm of concern in the biohacker community because it seemed to be the first step in a crackdown we all fear is coming.

Currently, no state has a law banning voluntary microchip implants, though along with Nevada, Arkansas, New Jersey and Tennessee are drafting legislation centered around implants. California, Wisconsin, Missouri, Oklahoma and North Dakota have laws in some form that ban involuntary implants.

I can't think of many biohackers — or any citizens — who wouldn't support a ban on involuntary microchipping (though at least for now, that's a baseless fear). But the fear of government- or corporate-imposed programs should not overwhelm the promise that voluntary, recreational chipping has to offer.

I've had my chip for over three years, and I've grown to relish and rely on the technology. The electric lock on the front door of my house has a chip scanner, and it's nice to go surfing and jogging without having to carry keys around.

For some people without functioning arms, chips in their feet are the simplest way to open doors or operate some household items modified with chip readers. The military is considering implants for soldiers that may be useful to monitor their health data and even recovering them if they're captured or lost in war.

Microchip implants aren't for everyone, and while the health risks are minuscule, like any technology, implanted chips will grow old, become outdated and need to be replaced — a process that will be moderately bloody and painful. And there are legitimate privacy issues, similar to the current concerns over tracking phones. So far, though, implants can be detected by someone only at a distance of a few feet.

Above all, the microchip implants illustrate a defining principle of the transhumanist movement, popularized by the philosopher and futurist Max More: morphological freedom — the right to modify one's body in whatever way one wants, so long as it doesn't hurt anybody else.

The uproar over Mr. Daly's bill seems to have worked. After being deluged with public comments and emails, he altered his bill yet again, with new wording to exempt implants for self-expression and medical purposes. (The bill recently passed in the Nevada Assembly and is being considered by the Nevada Senate.)

With implant technology becoming smaller and easier to put into bodies, every state will soon have to address the question of recreational implants. The knee-jerk opposition is real, and it could easily lead to overbearing laws. People should be able to do whatever they want with their bodies — and lawmakers, if they study the facts, will quickly realize that the benefits of a lightly regulated biohacking culture outweigh the risks.

****

2) The New Bionic Sports of the Future Transhumanist Olympics

A quiet revolution is happening in competitive sports. Some futurists think that in just decades, humans will sprint faster than horses, people will shoot guns with near-perfect accuracy using bionic eyes, and athletes will swim entire races without taking a breath.

Already, untainted urine samples have become as essential to top runners as their shoes. Brainy engineers have become as necessary to cyclists as their bikes. And the precise carbohydrate/protein ratio in meals consumed by swimmers the night before racing the 400-meter individual medley has become as important as flip turns.

The rapid advancement and implementation of science and technology are dramatically changing the human species and our activities. Sports cannot remain the same. Bionic augmentation, performance-enhancing drugs, and radical technological innovation are the keys to the coming sporting events increasingly being called transhumanist competition. The word "transhuman" literally means beyond human.

So far, society has had trouble with embracing radical science and technology in many competitive sports, especially those which heavily rely on physical performance of the human body. Instead of encouraging open usage of performance-enhancing drugs and technologies to evolve competition, most sporting bodies and their leadership have sharply condemned anything that deviates from the status quo competitive milieu of the first modern-day Olympics held in Athens, Greece. In 1896.

That may change as the benefits of transhumanist-minded competition become obvious to athletes and spectators alike.

"To some extent the Olympics and related sporting competition is about seeing how far the human being can go, how far it can perform," said Peter Rothman, a futurist, scientist, and editor at H+ Magazine. "Transhumanist competition and an Olympics dedicated to it would be the fullest expression of this idea."

If we fast-forward 20 years, what might such a cybernetic competition look like? Surely, it will be even more exciting than what we already have. Take one of the favorite winter Olympic sports, Freestyle Skiing—Aerial, where athletes slide down launch ramps of various lengths and hurl into the air performing multiple aerobatic feats. Two tricky issues define this dangerous sport: how much air time a skier can get and how badly the skier will be hurt if they don't land their jump safely. New technology, both of which are likely to be available in 5-10 years time, would handily deal with these issues.

First, lightweight mini-rocket thrusters attached to the back of skis would burn for a few seconds, pushing ski jumpers down launch ramps at far higher speeds than ever before. Naturally, the air-time of jumps will be far longer and higher than without the rockets. But it's the type of ski suit that these aerial skiers wear that would allow them to do tricks only futurists dream off.

Sensor-controlled suits could instantaneously inflate all around the body if the skier can't make a safe landing. Instead of breaking bones, the jumper would bounce down the slopes, unharmed but probably cursing. As far as aerial tricks go, with so much air time, expect newly invented ones. Instead of performing the Kangaroo Flip 900, expect the Toxic Rodeo 1620. Maybe throw in a few variations for kicks.

Regardless what happens in a coming Transhumanist Olympics, all sports will still need rules. Exoskeleton technology could soon allow unthinkable feats, say, swimmers running on water. Powerlifting would likely be a sport defined by super-enhancement muscle-building drugs, customized steroid treatments, bone strengtheners, and epinephrine-like shots that create short-lasting bursts of adrenaline and rage. Just enough to lift a ton of deadweight above one's head. Obviously, we'd need some safeguards here.

The sport of swimming might include webbing fingers together with skin grafts to give improved paddle-like effects. We could see sleek, no-drag, full-body suits and even aerodynamic helmets. Finally, an injectable short-term microparticle "oxygen substitute" would make races completely underwater where resistance is least. Swimming may become the first Olympic sport with no breathing.

The monetary incentive, along with the bonus of prestige, fame, and pride, has certainly pushed athletes to use radical science and technology to improve their performance. As with the exploits of Lance Armstrong and Alex Rodriguez, who used illegal performance-enhancing drugs to reach the top of their respective sports. Many others are using proven and legal, or questionable and illegal products and methods to improve their performance. Some athletes will do what they must to win.

In the face of the increasingly strict policing of athletes—the anti-progressive "war on performance-enhancing drugs"— a Transhumanist Olympics would be an outlet for experimentation beyond "natural" ability. It would be an alternative for athletes who dedicate much of their lives to a sport and don't want to be constantly scrutinized as potential cheaters and forced to undergo strip searches and urine tests right before events.

Today, you break a world record and the first thing someone wants from you is a blood sample, not a congratulatory high-five. Transhumanist competition could change that, embrace the science and technology that can make sporting events ever-more thrilling, and evolve athletic competition, finally, to fit the 21st century.

****

3) #TalktoMe: Futurist Zoltan Istvan Interviews his Aging Father

My mother and father illegally left communist Hungary in 1969 and came to America to start their lives afresh. Like hundreds of thousands of other Eastern Europeans living under the oppressive Soviet Union regime, my father wanted a better life. In America, he found what he was looking for and prospered.

Unfortunately, like billions of others, he has not been able to escape the ravages of aging. My father — aged 71 — has recently had his 4th heart attack, and he also contends with diabetes. Given his challenging health, I thought it was a good time to interview him on camera and get his thoughts on life — especially as I have chosen to focus my career and 2016 US presidential campaign on the growing field of life extension science and transhumanism.

In the interview, part of *The Huffington Post* "Talk To Me" video series, my father reveals a powerful fact — that the draw to come to America has much do with its promise of the American Dream. In the late 1960s, many Hungarians and people in communist countries found it amazing that the average American could own a car. At the time, such luxuries were deemed nearly impossible to Eastern Europeans except for the super rich. My father was always a lover of motorcycles, boats, recreational machines, and technology. He wanted his own car, and, of course, he got it in America — many of them. In fact, I grew up in California riding and racing motorcycles, since one of my father's great passions was enduro riding.

Here's our 7-minute video interview (transcribed) where I ask my father about his personal journey, his projections of the future, and his thoughts on my presidential campaign:

Zoltan (looking at camera before turning to father): Hello. My name is Zoltan Istvan Gyurko, and I'm the 2016 US presidential candidate for the Transhumanist Party. I'm doing an interview with my 71-year-old father Steven Gyurko as part of *The Huffington Post* Talk to Me series, and I'm really excited about it. I don't think we've ever actually done a formal sit-down interview, but so Father, tell me what year did you come from Hungary with Mom and what was it like? What was the drive to come to America?

Steven: From Hungary we came over here in 1969, and my brother-in-law—your Mom's brother—was living in United States at the time, and he came home and showed us some pictures that he had from America. Because living in Hungary, we simply didn't believe it the average American person could be capable of owning an automobile, and all through my life, I liked motorcycles and automobiles, so I said: We're going to go take a look, and sure enough, average Americans owned cars.

Zoltan: It must have been amazing since from Hungary, you've now been in America 30 or 40 years, and you've seen the state of technology, and the state of cars, and the state of sports change. I know you were a motorcycle rider for many years you even taught me how to do it in our enduro races. What do you think of how much everything has changed from where you grew up in Hungary to today in 2016?

Steven: Well, there are tremendous changes for sure. I don't even know how to describe it to you but that it is much wider than I ever thought it would be.

Zoltan: What do you think about my 2016 presidential campaign. Obviously I have no shot at winning but what do you think about me using the platform of technology, especially the platform to try to live a lot longer, because you know that's my main thing I've been trying to spread: that if America would spend its resources, we could probably conquer death sometime in the next 50 years or so. Well, at least we could make it so that people could live substantially longer. What do you think of that concept?

Steven: Well, I believe in this technology, because like it or not, it's going to be here, and you know stay, and there's gonna be even much more of it in the next five to ten years, so obviously they have possibilities on that side of things.

Zoltan: So you've had four heart attacks and you know you're 71 years old, have diabetes; you've had certain amounts of serious disease in your life and you're getting older, and let's be honest: one of the reasons I want to do this interview is because I was not sure how much longer you're going to live. Do you think that if you could live another five or ten years they might be able to fix some of the things that are wrong with you right now like especially the heart and stuff like that? Maybe a robotic heart? Or is that still 20 to 30 years out?

Steven: I would say that parts like a heart and lung, they'll be able to fix something to improve it, but unfortunately our biggest problem is our plumbing, far as I know. We have 60,000 mile of blood vessels in our body and if those are plugged up, I can't see how they could fix up. I think it will take a long time to find some kind of a solution that makes sure they can unplug whatever is blocked, and my problem is that most of us plugged.

Zoltan: Now what are your some of your thoughts on dying? Like I mean, you're not a religious person, so what do you think happens? Or what do you generally think about death?

Steven: Well, you know when you're not physically your best, or not even close to it, it's sometimes almost like dying is a solution to the problem rather than worry about it. So, I'm not afraid of dying.

Zoltan: So, what do you think so far about your life? I mean, in general, you've had what I would call sort of an "American Dream" life. You came from Hungary, did well in business, you had two kids and they're healthy; they all have healthy kids of their own you know, so you have five grandkids. And you're still married to Mom, who I think is a great, great woman. So you've done I feel like really well in life, especially because you've had some friends die recently, and other tragedies have occurred to them, you know, and I think you've done really good to be honest. No in fact I think you've done great. Actually, you even have a son running for President, so let's see if maybe in eight years it will actually happen if I'm in a bigger campaign. But do you feel like your life went well?

Steve: Absolutely yes, so it's one of the reasons I'm not concerned about dying. Because I reflect on my life, and everything what I wanted to do, I did. You know I have airplanes, countless boats, and many motorcycles, and I was using them a lot. So I did have a good life; this country was good for me, that's for sure.

Zoltan: Well, Dad thank you for doing this interview. That's the end of the interview for *The Huffington Post* Talk to Me series, but it's been great to do this so we now have a formal record, and hopefully maybe we can get that technology to make you younger before you die. I'm working on it for both you and mom.

****

4) Cybernetics: More Transhuman than Human; Rumination on Cybernetic Technology

Are you ready for the future? A Transhumanist future in which everyone around you—friends, family, and neighbors—has dipped into the cybernetic punch bowl? This is a future of contact lenses that see in the dark, endoskeleton artificial limbs that lift a half-ton, and brain chip implants that read your thoughts and instantly communicate them to others. Sound crazy? Indeed, it does. Nevertheless, it's coming soon. Very soon. In fact, much of the technology already exists. It's being sold commercially at your local superstore or being tested in laboratories right now around the world.

We've all heard about driverless test cars on the roads and how doctors in France are replacing people's hearts with permanent robotic ones, but did you know there's already a multi-billion dollar market for brainwave-reading headsets? Using electroencephalography (EEG) sensors that pick up and monitor brain activity, NeuroSky's MindWave can attach to Google Glass and allow you to take a picture and post it to Facebook and Twitter just by thinking about it. Other headsets allow you to play video games on your iPhone with only your thoughts as well. In fact, a few months ago, the first mind-to-mind communication took place. A researcher in India projected a thought to a colleague in France, and using their headsets, they understood each other. Telepathy went from science fiction to reality, just like that.

The history of cybernetics—sometimes used to describe robotic implants, prosthetics, and cyborg-like enhancements in the human being and its experience—has come a long way since scientists began throwing around the term in the 1950s. What a difference a generation or two makes. Today a thriving pro-cyborg medical industry is setting the stage for trillion-dollar markets that will remake the human experience. Five million people in America suffer from Alzheimer's, but a new surgery that involves installing brain implants is showing promise in restoring people's memory and improving lives. The use of medical and microchip implants, whether in the brain or not, are expected to surge in the coming years. NBC News recently reported that many Americans will likely have chip implants within a decade's time. It's truly a new age for humans.

Standing proud at the forefront of all this change is the fascinating biohacker culture, where extreme inventors and innovators are leading the way by sticking RFID tracking chips in their bodies, permanent wireless headphones near their eardrums, and magnets in their fingers.

Rich Lee, a leading biohacker—also called a "grinder"—told me that "Implanting magnets in your fingertips gives you the ability to feel magnetic fields. Your fingertips have lots of nerve endings jammed into one area and they are really sensitive to stimuli. Magnets twitch or move in the presence of magnetic fields, and when you implant one in your finger you can really start to feel different magnetic fields around you. So it is like a sixth sense. You can now perceive an otherwise invisible world."

Of course, the challenge with such progress is the question of whether we're leaving behind our humanness and humanity. It's a good question. However, we shouldn't forget our sense of being a human is ultimately based on millions of years of evolution. In the end, like it or not, we are still stardust from eons ago—and not just biological humans. Perhaps deep down, the essence of our being and the wiring of our brain comprehend that in a spiritual way we can't rationally understand yet. After all, our evolutionary heritage is the cornerstone of why human beings are what they are: mammals that are becoming gods.

Whatever happens, along the way humans and their advancing technology will create paths and designs of our universe that transform us into other entities—into transhuman beings. We are standing at the doorstep of a new world and experience, and the cybernetic punch bowl is just our first drink of the future.

****

5) A TEDx Talk Celebrating Scientists and Exploring the Technological Future of Beauty

I recently was the closing speaker at the 5th annual TEDxTransmedia event, held in Geneva, Switzerland. My speech was titled *The Beauty of Being Alive*, and the first half of that talk has already been published here at *The Huffington Post*. But now I wanted to share the second part, which explores the people I consider the most beautiful in the world. It also discusses the future of beauty as we progress into a more technologically advanced and digital world. Here's the condensed version of the second half of the speech:

While I have already told you about my most beautiful experience in life, I also want to tell you about the people I consider the most beautiful in the world. Given my passion for transhumanism, I'm betting you can guess who those people are. To me, scientists, researchers, and those in medicine are the most beautiful people in the world. In fact, those scientists, researchers, and health professionals who work on keeping all of us alive are all brilliant works of art themselves. They are the true artists of the universe, constantly working on a masterpiece: a healthier, stronger species. They have spent their lives working hard to make our lives longer, better, and happier.

I want to tell you about one very special and beautiful person I know very well. She is my wife. She is also a board certified, fellowship trained medical doctor. Her specialty is Obstetrics and Gynecology. When I asked her what one of her most beautiful moments in life was, she answered a single name: Mombasa. The legendary city in Kenya.

After many years of doing scientific research and finishing various graduate degrees (which also included a 4-year US medical degree) my wife took an extended trip to Mombasa to work in one of the largest, most chaotic public hospitals in Kenya. Mombasa suffers from an incredibly high rate of HIV infection, and many women my wife treated were pregnant rape victims, cervical cancer patients, and post-partum hemorrhage cases.

My wife told me the most touching experience of her two months in Mombasa was treating a 16-year-old girl who developed a dangerous infection in her uterus after suffering through a miscarriage. Unfortunately, at the time in Mombasa, there was little state money for antibiotics in this hospital. Responsibility was often on the patient to attain their own medications. But this poor girl had no family, no resources, and no money whatsoever to buy the antibiotics. She was going to die. My wife walked across the street outside the hospital, as she sometimes did for her other patients, and bought the life saving medications for the teenage girl from a private pharmacy. She was able to save and heal the girl. What makes this story even more wonderful is my wife wasn't the only doctor buying medicines for their patients. Many other foreign and African doctors were also doing it to keep their patients alive if the patients couldn't afford it.

Retelling this story, I can't help but believe that those people that work to preserve our lives and health — in whatever capacity they do it — are the most beautiful people on the planet.

The end of my speech is nearing. And what I want to leave you with is a glimpse of future beauty. Future beauty is synonymous with exponential technology. Future beauty is going to be so revolutionary that many of us will find it hard to even imagine now. We are here in the flesh today, but beauty will likely not be flesh in 50 or a 100 years time. Beauty will likely be something synthetic. You will be part synthetic. We will all be part synthetic. We will be cyborgs. Our bodies will be made of materials none of us have even seen before. Some of our minds may be made entirely of microprocessors. Our thoughts will be able to be deciphered by 1s and 0s. In fact, we may not even be physical anymore. We may live entirely in machines, as avatars of our former selves, or as whatever creations we want. We will be truly different beings than humans, and on our way to the singularity, the most potentially beautiful event in the history of civilization

Experts say the Earth is a few billions years old and the universe is approximately 13.6 billions years old. Such numbers are astronomical and beyond the true grasp of our current human emotional comprehension. Like you, I stand at awe of this marvel of time and life that we experience here on Earth. I stand at awe at the gargantuan miracle of the universe, and the tiny collection of star dust we all are as we watch our species evolve. But I also stand triumphant as a human being ready to change and morph into something far different than we've ever been. I stand secure and optimistic that the future will be better than the past, and the quickening direction of human evolution is an important and brilliant journey. I stand secure that we will soon overcome human death and become truly the godlike entities that our species was meant to become.

Yet, whatever happens to all of us, whatever happens to all of our lives, to be alive is to be beautiful. And the most beautiful thing we can do in the universe is to continue being alive.

****

6) Will Brain Wave Technology Eliminate the Need for a Second Language?

Earlier this year, the first mind-to-mind communication took place. Hooked up to brain wave headsets, a researcher in India projected a thought to a colleague in France, and they understood each other. Telepathy went from the pages of science fiction to reality.

Using electroencephalography (EEG) sensors that pick up and monitor brain activity, brain wave technology has been advancing quickly in the last few years. A number of companies already sell basic brain wave reading devices, such as the Muse headband. Some companies offer headsets that allow you to play a video game on your iPhone using only thoughts. NeuroSky's MindWave can attach to Google Glass and allow you to take a picture and post it to Facebook and Twitter just by thinking about it. Even the army has (not very well) flown a helicopter using only thoughts and a brain wave headset.

Despite the immense interest in brain wave technology, little attention has been paid to what translation apps—such as Google Translator—will mean to an upcoming generation that will likely embrace brain wave tech. Youth will surely ask: What is the point of learning a second language if everyone will be communicating with brain wave headsets that can perform perfect real-time language translations?

The question is valid, even if it's sure to upset millions of second language teachers and dozens of language learning companies, like publicly traded Rosetta Stone. Like it or not, sophisticated brain wave headsets will soon become as cheap as cell phones. A growing number of technologists think the future of communication lies in these headsets, and not handheld devices or smart phones.

However, the question of whether it will be useful to learn a new language in the future is about far more than just human communication and what technological form that takes.

Different languages introduce us to other cultures, other peoples, and other countries. This creates personal growth, offering invaluable examination on our own culture and how we perceive the world. The process broadens who we are.

Being proficient in other languages also offers certain nuances that knowing only one language cannot. French offers far more romantic and poetic gist than English ever can. But Arabic is steeped in more historical imagery and connotation than French. And nothing compares to Hungarian's ability to effectively curse in ways that all other languages fall far short of.

Perhaps most importantly, learning a second language offers the physical brain a chance to grow in new and meaningful ways. The study of a new language, for example, is often suggested to early on-set Alzheimer's patients to help stimulate the brain's proper functioning.

Ultimately, the most quintessential question rests on whether there are more important things to be doing in today's busy world than learning a new language. With radical transhumanist tech changing our most basic functions like communicating, is society better off pushing its youth to learn how to write code, or to speed read, or to play the violin? In hindsight, I would've rather spent my time becoming a proficient martial artist than the six years I studied Spanish in school.

Whatever your opinion, the future of learning languages and how we communicate is in flux. Speaking at the 2014 World Future Society conference in Florida, Singularity University Professor Jose Cordeiro said, "Spoken language could start disappearing in 20 years. We'll all talk with each other using thoughts scanned and projected from our headsets and maybe even chip implants. This will radically increase the speed and bandwidth of human communications."

Twenty years isn't that far off. I'm not ready yet to drop my 4-year-old daughter's Chinese lessons, but I am keeping my eye on whether technology is going to change some of our basic communication assumptions, like the value of learning a second language.

****

7) *Quartz*: We Asked Some of the Boldest Thinkers What the World will be like in 50 Years. Here's what Zoltan Istvan Told Us

QZ: Who will run the world?

Zoltan: The world will be run by AI networks and networks of quantum intelligence. Nations will have ceased to exist as independent physical entities because they will be online and have all merged as one. Humans may exist, but they will be off the AI grid, and contributing very little to progress and what is happening to the world.

QZ: Which country will have the most powerful economy?

Countries won't exist in a formal way. Economies won't exist either, except those of people who didn't choose to merge their brains with AI. But the real scale of intelligence and progress will all be done in the online clouds and around the universe as quantum intelligence.

QZ: What kinds of companies will be the most important?

Zoltan: Those humans who join AI and merge their brains directly with machines won't work, but will live in virtual worlds freely. Those humans that don't merge with AI will have companies whose primary goal is to keep AI out of the lives of the rest of the humans left on the planet.

QZ: What will cause the biggest conflicts?

Zoltan: A conflict of who merges with AI and who doesn't is coming. It will likely be a civil war of sorts. Ultimately, people won't be able to stop progress, and most humans will upload themselves into new worlds where they don't die, don't have to work, or live as biological beings who suffer.

QZ: How will people earn a living?

Zoltan: If you are uploaded to a cloud, you won't have to earn a living. You will give up some control of your life, and that will be your payment into this world to exist. It will be a near-perfect world of bliss and progress.

QZ: How will we communicate with each other?

Zoltan: Communication will be only through thoughts. Nothing else will exist for those that are uploaded into the cloud or live in quantum intelligence enclaves.

QZ: What will we eat?

Zoltan: There will be no eating, no breathing, no drinking, no using the bathroom. The flesh will be gone, paving the way for the exploration of how intelligent we can become.

QZ: How will we die?

Zoltan: There will be no death, even if we want to die. We will be able to turn ourselves off for periods of time, but even through quantum archaeology, we may be recreated many times, in many realities.

QZ: How will we find love?

Zoltan: Love in a romantic way will cease to exist. We will only be willing to communicate with the nearly all-knowing AI that we are connected to—which, in fact, is one with us. However, this AI will be connected to everyone else too, so we will always be interconnected in a sort of hive mind.

QZ: How will we get information?

Zoltan: We will constantly build out networks and use of the quantum world outward. This will increase our intelligence all the time, every moment. That is the real goal of this new world—as much power and intelligence as possible. We must conquer the universe.

QZ: What forms of transportation will we use?

Zoltan: Our minds and thoughts will travel at the speed of light, using networks of computer chips.

QZ: What will cities be like?

Zoltan: There will only be one city in the uploaded world, the great AI city of minds.

QZ: What will our borders be like?

Zoltan: There will be no borders, except the ability to sabotage the AI and quantum intelligence enclaves themselves. This will not be permitted.

QZ: Will we have ventured to other planets?

Zoltan: Yes, there will be humans left that have traveled to live and procreate on other planets. In case our great experiment with uploading ourselves to the cloud fails, we will still have our species to carry on and try again.

QZ: What will our most valuable resource be?

Zoltan: Our ability to reason. If we can think, we are alive. But if we have lost that ability, all is lost.

QZ: What will the biggest change to our natural world be?

Zoltan: People will come to realize that nature and the material world are harsh, and the world technologists are trying to bring will be one without suffering.

QZ: Will our world be more equal or less equal?

Zoltan: There will be great inequality between humans and those who have uploaded themselves.

QZ: What technology will bring about the biggest change in society?

Zoltan: Neural implants that are so good we can transfer our consciousness to a computer in full form.

QZ: What's your best prediction for the world in 50 years?

Zoltan: A great transhumanist war will occur between those who embrace radical technology in their bodies and those who don't. Many will be affected by this time, and some will call it the end times. Those that side with technology and AI will win.

****

CHAPTER II: DIVING DEEPER

8) The 5 Most Revolutionary Scientific Trends to Look Out For (2017)

2016 was a powerful year for science and technology innovation. CRISPR gene editing technology became nearly a household name with its potential to affect humanity. SpaceX rockets landed themselves. And a baby was born with three parents.

But what's in store for 2017?

While some decry the developed world is falling apart due to changing political environments, science and technology innovation is likely to continue thriving. In fact, innovation is occurring so fast, I believe 2017 will be the year governments begin to consider forming new science, technology, and futurist agencies and organizations to better contend with the rapid change. The old ones are mired in bureaucracy, conservative religious ideology, and the past—unable to contend with issues like nanotechnology, artificial intelligence, and virtual reality. Borrowing from *The Wizard of Oz*, "We're not in Kansas anymore."

Let's take a look at the top five developments I anticipate for 2017:

1) Neural prosthetics—the idea we can benefit greatly by connecting our thoughts directly to the computing power of machines—will become the holy grail of human progress.

Artificial intelligence and robotics are developing so quickly that in the next decade, I believe they'll take away approximately 25 million jobs in America from humans. In case you don't know how many jobs that is, that's about three times as many jobs as was lost during the recent Great Recession in the US.

America should look at natural disasters and past wartime scenarios to get an idea of how disruptive AI and robotics will be to the economy. Already, the world's largest hedge fund is creating tech to replace its workers with machine intelligence in less than five years time. Don't expect Wall Street to have human workers in 10 years time, unless they can somehow upgrade themselves.

That's where neural prosthetics comes in. It's a technology that can and might keep humans competitive indefinitely. These so-called brain readers and communicators will allow humans to utilize AI—in real time cognition—for its own intelligence. After all, what's better than a super smart human mind? A super smart human mind directly connected to a super smart artificial intelligence.

Personally, I love this idea. And I have volunteered to be a test subject of implants and headsets that read brain waves. My senior thesis in college was on brains in a vat, and the idea of being a part of the Matrix fascinates me.

The use of neural prosthetics will change human nature, but without it, I doubt humans can be competitive in the future to machine labor. Besides without human labor, there's no guarantee capitalism, as we know it, can survive. After all, capitalism is based on human labor, and if machines do everything, then it's likely to end up a very different economic system.

Almost by default, to keep humans competitive in the labor force, we'll have to become transhuman—and utilize radical technology as intrinsic parts of our bodies. Otherwise, only the very rich will own robotics and AI companies, leaving the rest of us in a jobless dystopia.

One company called Kernel, which launched this year with a 100 million dollars of the founders own money, tech visionary Bryan Johnson, is leading the way. I expect many more startups to join the fray in 2017.

2) President-elect Trump will hire an anti-red tape FDA chief that streamlines the Food and Drug Administration, making more drugs available to save lives and improve health.

No matter how you look at it, the FDA has become a bureaucracy monster. Early in 2016, I wrote about this FDA problem in *Motherboard*:

"On average, a new drug takes at least 10 years from creation to arrival in your cabinet in America. Additionally, Matthew Herper at *Forbes* reports that about $5 billion is spent on average developing a new drug. New medical devices—especially those life saving ones—take upwards of seven years to hit the market. For patients, some who are dying to get the drugs and devices, this may as well be an eternity. Nearly all of this has to do with the FDA and the bureaucratic labyrinth that exists to make sure medicine is safe in America.

Now don't get me wrong, I also want safe medicine. And for the most part, the FDA does that. But sometimes there are more important things than safe medicine, especially if you're suffering from a debilitating and terminal disease. For example, many people believe access to medicine before they die is more important than whether that medicine is safe or not. And with such a long, laborious, and costly medical approval process in the US, many inventors and companies that would like to create new medicine don't do it because of the prohibitive procedure of bearing a product from conception to sale."

One such choice for FDA Chief being floated around by media outlets is free market-minded Jim O'Neill, managing director for Mithril Capital, which was cofounded by Peter Thiel. Mr. O'Neill, who formerly worked in the George W. Bush administration, would be just the kind of person to cut the fat off the FDA and get America better drugs for better health.

3) Driverless cars will appear in all major American cities, challenging state and local laws.

This month Uber was in my hometown of San Francisco, testing out its new driverless vehicles. After several reports of driverless cars running red lights, the California DMW quickly shut it down, sending it packing to Arizona where laws are more favorable.

I found this sad, as did many techno-optimists. Being in driverless cars is one of the more visceral experiences people can have that make them understand the transhumanist age has indeed arrived. Driverless cars will be a philosophical turning point for many Americans, many who are not sure they really believe the future will be automation-ubiquitous.

But like California, some governments—often led by luddite lobbyists and general fear—will resist, setting up the stage for US Congress to consider the matter. At some point, the Supreme Court may even have to get involved to okay such change. The facts are the transportation industry will be completely different animal within 10 years time. And 2017 will be the year local governments rise up to grapple with the coming driverless world.

4) Life Extension science will go mainstream with multiple science breakthroughs and new companies joining the quest for the "Fountain of Youth"

2016 was a banner year or the life extension industry. Even Mark Zuckerberg came out and established his own multi-billion dollar commitment with the goal of curing, preventing, or managing all human disease by the end of the century. The rise of CRISPR genetic editing further gave the movement new firepower as the possibility to rewrite our very own genetic code—including our hereditary shortcoming and the aging process—became not just possible, but plausible. Finally, events like the thousand-person life extension-oriented RAAD Festival, the Longevity Cookbook, and my own Immortality Bus made headlines as America wondered aloud what indefinite lifespans meant—and how it might affect humanity.

Despite that, we still live in a country with strong deathist attitudes. Ironically, I suspect that life extension will become much more well known in a Republican controlled-government, as the conflict between religious values and science allowing us to live indefinitely ultimately reach a climax, one that will end up in civil strife and Congressional discussion.

I've said this on my presidential campaign trail before: The more people that label transhumanism as something dangerous, the more popular it'll become. That's human nature for you.

5) Because many leaders in the incoming Trump Administration don't believe in climate change, scientists will change their focus from carbon footprint prevention to radical geoengineering tech to save the planet.

As a journalist who's traveled extensively to write more than a dozen environmental stories—many for National Geographic—I've seen some of the Earth's destruction firsthand. I've witnessed the decimation of millions of hectares of Paraguay's forests. I've seen major oil spills in the ocean. And as a Communications Director at nonprofit WildAid I've searched for extremely endangered species in Southeast Asia—some that are simply no longer there.

It's sad what we as a people have done to Planet Earth. But we will rebuild. And I believe we will make Earth more plentiful and beautiful than ever before. How? With radical technology that is right now being created in laboratories around the world.

In just 10 years time, I believe we may have the ability through genetic editing to regrow rainforests at 5-10 times their normal speed of growth—giving us the power to replenish the damaged Amazon basin. We already have some of the Jurassic Park tech to bring back endangered species like the Siamese Crocodile in Cambodia, where just about 400 remain in the wild. And we already have ways to do basic engineering on our climate. Rain is not something sent from the "gods," but the precise mixture of certain weather and atmospheric conditions, as China is already experimenting with. We are learning how to make it. We can be the new generation of rain makers—or of endless sunny days (though presumably we'd want a mixture of both).

Perhaps, the leading green tech will be nanotechnology—where we can literally remake the planet to our taste. This type of tech involves affecting and building matter and objects on a molecular level. In line with this tech are ways of consuming pollution or even garbage—the hope is we can create nanobots that eat the waste and pollution humans have made. Already, researchers are experimenting with fungi that eat plastic.

Transhumanism is the key to making the Earth pristine again, not forcing people to make less of a carbon footprint. While I believe in respecting the Earth and not polluting it, the future of beautifying nature belongs more to technology and science than human restraint. That said, my techno-optimism knows that geoengineering presents risks too, as we would be in uncharted territory. We must be careful not to create unintended long term consequences of our environment we can't reverse.

Despite challenges, I'm betting 2017 is the year scientists, technologists, engineers, and the public begin to openly accept geoengineering as a leading way to fulfill goals of the environmental movement. In the face of an American government and leadership that largely is not interested in climate change, the best way forward is likely through radical science and technology innovation.

****

9) The First International Beauty Contest Judged by Robots

Robots are starting to appear everywhere: driving cars, cooking dinners and even as robotic pets.

But people don't usually give machine intelligence much credence when it comes to judging beauty. That may change with the launch of the world's first international beauty contest judged exclusively by a robot jury.

The contest, which requires participants to take selfies via a special app and submit them to the contest website, is touting new sophisticated facial recognition algorithms that allow machines to judge beauty in new and improved ways.

The contest intends to have robots analyze the many age-related changes on the human face and evaluate the impact on perception of these changes by people of various ages, races, ethnicities and nationalities.

Dr. Alex Zhavoronkov, a consultant on the competition and CEO of Insilco Medicine, a bioinformatics company focusing on aging research, says "Recent advances in Deep Learning have made machine recognition of beauty aspects far better than ever before."

Machine intelligence capabilities have been steadily growing in sophistication every year. Some experts say Moore's Law — where a microchip doubles in computing power about every 24 months — may not hold up as well as it has in the last two decades. However, even if Moore's Law fails in the future, new methods of computing, like quantum computing, may again set the industry on breakneck development speeds.

Part of the AI beauty contest framework is not just for humans submitting selfies, but also programmers submitting their best algorithms for machine detection of beauty. Near the bottom of the contest website is a link for algorithm submissions that takes coders to a page saying, "Would you like to go down in history as one of the first data scientists who taught a machine to estimate human attractiveness?" In a way, this makes the contest a crowd-sourced event.

Of course, getting robots to understand beauty is not just for kicks. Behind the motive is a massive anti-aging industry that wants to better understand how youthfulness can be better monitored and implemented. I suspect it's part of the reason Microsoft, Nvidia, Youth Laboratories and other companies are prominently listed on the website as "partners and supporters."

"This contest will help build impartial feature-specific and general robots that will help us understand our faces. But my personal dream is to have this contest extended into anti-aging and general healthcare space," said Nastya Georgievskaya, robot tutor at Youth Laboratories, a company developing deep learning systems for facial analysis.

Dr. Zhavoronkov told me the contest hopes to facilitate the launch of a series of apps that will allow people to track the effects of various products (including cosmetics) on their face — ones that quickly allow them to understand the impact on perception using impartial opinion of deep-learned algorithms.

"People may not care about how to extend their lifespans, but they definitely care about the way they look," Zhavoronkov wrote me. "Insilco Medicine used massive multi-omics data from academic and commercial partnerships to predict the likely geroprotectors that may have beneficial effects on human skin, and we need a way to test the efficacy of these interventions. We will be launching an application called RYNKL in the coming weeks if all goes well, which will allow users to take standardized selfies periodically to analyze the changes in 'wrinkleness' of their face in the context of their lifestyle, behavior, and other interventions."

This beauty contest will run every half a year, and more and more teams from all over the world will be invited to try their robots on human faces linked to multiple other parameters. The overriding goal of the contest is discover complex rating systems that will teach machines to evaluate humans, which will be important to getting robots to act more like us — and also to understand our ways. Of course, humans may be in for a surprise if machines decide many of us are not attractive — or are even downright ugly.

Alex Shevtsov, founder and CEO of Youth Laboratories, recently asked, "You may like your Tesla, but would you like your Tesla to like you?"

Despite the competition featuring the next generation of machine recognition, the beauty contest does not allow participants to use make-up, have beards or wear hats in their submitted selfies. Maybe in a few years, that will be worked out, so machines will be able to understand more than skin-deep beauty, but also human's love of endless and often artistic material accessories, like earings, fancy dresses and even tattoos.

Eventually, through this technology, machines may even learn to judge another machine's appearance, opening up the possible world of robot attraction and love.

****

10) Major Transhumanism Conference Features Both Rising and Seasoned Experts

On March 21st, nonprofit organization Brighter Brains Institute held the first major US transhumanism conference of the year, located in San Jose, California. Titled Transhuman Strategies, the conference was host to an exciting array of speakers. Notably different from other transhumanist conferences before was the blend of both young and seasoned transhumanists, a sure sign that the science and technology advocating movement is growing among a younger demographic. *Vice Motherboard* had a 4-person film crew on hand to capture the event, adding to the excitement that transhumanism is continuing to break into the mainstream.

The conference talks were centered on four key questions:

What are the Transhuman Goals in the near future?

How can these Transhuman ideas permeate the mainstream?

Are there ways Transhumanism can assert itself in the political sphere?

How can Transhumanist ideas and innovations create a better world now, for billions of people on Earth?

With nearly 100 people in attendance, speakers attempted to address the questions in their own way while emphasizing their field of expertise. Digital iconoclast RU Sirius and his writing partner, Lifeboat Foundation advisor Jay Cornell, gave talks and signed copies of their new book *Transcendence: The Disinformation Encyclopedia of Transhumanism and the Singularity*. British philosopher, lecturer, and entrepreneur Riva-Melissa Tez spoke on bettering transhumanist strategies. Russian scientist Maria Konovalenko and businessman Mikhail Batin spoke on transhumanism activism in the field of longevity. Futurist and CEO of The Foresight Company John Smart spoke on foresight development and how to attain the best future. *H+ Magazine* editor and computer engineer Peter Rothman discussed ways to help get funding for transhumanist projects. Adam Marblestone, "Director of Scientific Architecting" with the Synthetic Neurobiology group at MIT, spoke on new strategies to accelerate brain science. Hank Pellissier, the organizer of the event, spoke on the emerging concept of transhumanitarianism — where transhumanists do humanitarian deeds with an emphasis on using science and technology for the greater good.

I spoke on how transhumanism has been recently entering the political arena. Increasingly, futurists are hoping that through politics, radical science and technology will gain a better foothold in society. Some of the questions I brought up in my speech apply to all Americans. For example: How will Hillary Clinton address the growing concerns of Designer Babies, now that the technology is just a few years away? What about Jeb Bush (who carries the stem cell research moratorium stigma of his older brother)? Presumably, conservatives like newly announced US Presidential candidate Ted Cruz would seek to limit such advances in technology that could turn future children into potential superhumans, even if it's in the best interest of the species' health.

Of course, not all science and technology are safe. Even amongst the transhumanist community, many aren't sure what the outcome of creating a superintelligent AI will bring. Will we use its incredible possibilities to transform the species to ever greater heights? Or will an independent AI seek to destroy us in some Terminator scenario?

Whatever happens, the quickly growing field of transhumanism and its advocates are searching out the answers right now. Some people in America might not be ready yet for some of the progressive ideas transhumanists present, but the growth of radical science and technology in our world seems inevitable. The best way to handle such change in the way humans live and evolve with technology is to make a powerful effort to understand it all far ahead of time. Conferences like Transhuman Strategies — especially when they include a broad swath of age groups, perspectives, and nationalities in their speakers — are a good start in trying to address the issues in our changing world.

****

11) Is College Worth It? What Would You Have Paid to Get Your Degree?

A young supporter of my futurist work asked me the other day if going to college and getting a degree was worth the increasingly large price tag in countries where college is not free. I answered: *Yes*. In fact, I would've paid five times the amount I paid for college to get my undergrad degree.

With so much oppressive college debt out there causing anti-education vibes, mine is an unpopular opinion—especially among millennials and Gen Zers buried under school loans. But I've found my degree has opened up so many doors that it's become invaluable to me.

I studied Philosophy and Religion in college, and I've never formally used my degree in a way that fundamentally taps the knowledge of those subjects. But coming from immigrant parents who didn't even finish formal high school in Communist Hungary, I believe a college degree is more an identifier—something we draw and lean on for identity throughout our life.

For example, being a college grad was important for my wife when we met on Match.com. It was the same for me with her. Her profile didn't have a picture with it, but it had lots of initials behind her name. I was interested. People age, wrinkles appear, and skin sags, but degrees last forever.

One way to measure success in this world is in to see a family line's upward climb trying to reach the Western dream of becoming wealthy. Each generation getting more education is generally a good measure. Just about every statistic out there says that graduating from college leaves people happier, more prosperous, married longer, and healthier.

Both my wife and I paid for the majority of our educations ourselves. We took out various loans and had education price tags in the six figures each, some which we still pay.

While I'd love to find a way to fund free public college across the country for anyone who wants it—such as Europe has—such a financial freebie is unlikely to be passed while we have a split US Congress.

In the meantime, prospective students (and their parents if they're lucky) must ask how much they are willing to pay to get a higher education degree. My wife is a medical doctor who trained in higher education for 19 years before receiving her first real paycheck. When I asked her how much she would've paid for her education, she told me she'd have paid at least twice what she did.

Of course, a lot of her answer—as well as the reason I loved college—has nothing to do with choice of career or how high one's salary is later in life. College is an experience. A lot of first-time things happen there—and these are things that probably will only happen during this specific short period of one's life. Only half of college, I'd surmise, is about academics. There's an enormous amount of social change and growth that occurs outside of the books. Of course, I'm talking about sex, drugs, and rock-n-roll (or whatever music is popular today). It's a great time to be alive while soaking in a plethora of new ideas, friends and experiences.

People say college is expensive. However, the most expensive choice I usually see people making is not attempting to go to college because of prohibitive costs. I suggest finding a way to attend, even if it means taking out loans, getting grants, begging family, and working part time during one's education, as I often did.

Most importantly, to make college positively worthwhile, I advocate for people to study something they love. That way they'll never be disappointed in the journey of getting a college education.

****

12) The Augmented Expo in San Jose was Fascinating

A few months ago, I was invited by tech guru Tom Emrich to speak at the Augmented World Expo in San Jose. The event, nicknamed on posters Superpowers to the People, took place on June 1st and 2nd. Billed as the largest virtual reality, augmented reality, and wearable tech event, the expo didn't disappoint. It was massive and filled with excited techies enjoying themselves. In fact, with over 200 exhibits and gadgets to experiment with—like various kinds of reality headsets—the biggest problem was actually remembering all the amazing companies and their great products. There simply was too many of them.

Because this was my first presidential campaign event for a while in my home town of San Francisco—and I was being filmed by four film crews—I brought my wife and two daughters to the expo. At ages two and five, my kids were a handful, but they had lots of fun being part of the filming and seeing what the exhibits offered.

Later, I gave a keynote speech called *Virtual and Augmented Realities will Become the Future of Politics* on the main stage. It discussed how the presidential election will be different in 2020 vs. now in 2016. In short, expect Hillary or Trump drones carrying bumper stickers, candidates appearing in holographic forms at rallies, and dozens of driverless campaign buses touring the country. Expect more campaigning in virtual reality too, as well as cheering robot supporters. I'm ahead of other candidates in this regard, as I often tour around with a 4-foot robot named Jethro Knights. BBC's Dave Lee did a nice write up on some of the aspects of my expo speech in a fun titled article: *HoloTrump and the Future of Elections.*

CCTV, China's public TV, was also there at the Augmented World Expo. Journalist Mark Niu covered my presidential campaign and transhumanist views on longevity and artificial intelligence. Both CCTV-America and global CCTV English featured the expo in their daily news and business shows. The videos are fun watching.

Having been to many tech expos and conferences in the last few years, my takeaway from the Augmented World Expo is that the fields of virtual and augmented reality are growing faster than most people realize. It seems every time I strap on a new headset to test out these realities, they significantly improve. I can't wait for next year.

****

13) Think Driverless Cars Will be Modern-looking and Reduce Traffic. Think Again

I'm cruising around the country on my nearly 40-foot long "Immortality Bus" that's decked out to looks like a giant coffin. It's my brazen attempt to get attention to my third party presidential campaign, and fortunately, the wacky bus is doing its job. On the Golden Gate Bridge, in rush hour, hundreds of people are staring at it, and some are honking and yelling. My website is painted on the bus in big letters, and you can watch the hits to the website literally rise anytime I'm in traffic.

Signs.com, a Utah-based company with 85 employees, reports on its website: "According to the Outdoor Advertising Association of America, it is estimated that during an average day, a car advertisement can reach up to 70,000 impressions. That's a lot of eyeballs! In fact, vehicle advertising reaches more people than billboards, radio, direct mail, local group mailers and mass transit advertising. "

What does this have to do with driverless cars not being modern looking and causing more traffic? Lots.

There's a moment in time coming when driverless cars will become cheap enough—perhaps because of solar power or far more efficient batteries—to send them out in rush hour traffic simply to advertise. Covered totally in ads, these "spam cars" will justify operational and maintenance costs. And they will drive endlessly, making money for their owners from advertising sales.

Naturally, every major company (and probably nonprofit and government organizations too) will buy a fleet of these ad cars to do this. Surely, the automobile industry will experience a new boom.

But there's more. Why buy a normal car—with heated seats, radios, and air conditioning—that will never have drivers in it? In fact, why not produce a car for a soda company that looks like a can of soda? Look, there goes a Pepsi car! Or the Heinz ketchup vehicle. Or the Oscar Meyer Wiener bus. There go a hundred of them—all driving themselves around the country.

The road may soon look like a Walmart coupon page.

So far, this ad-car stuff rarely happens in the real world because it's not cost effective. But when that changes—and it may start in as soon as 10 years time—expect a whole new generation of cars (some maybe just totally covered in television screens) to be ubiquitous and to cruise everywhere.

Of course, with such an influx of advert vehicles on the road, normal drivers will experience traffic everywhere that resembles the 405 Freeway at 5 PM in Los Angeles—considered by millions one of the most aggravating experiences on Earth. The thing with ad vehicles is they are designed to make you pay attention to it, instead of the road. And that will help create more accidents and congestion.

That's probably why ad vehicles will soon be a major point of contention, reaching all the way to the US Congress, who will have to decide to allow them or not, and in what capacity.

In America, you can paint most anything you want on a car body, and even on some nonessential windows, depending on the state. Additionally, companies like My Free Car use vinyl cast to cover people's cars who drive for them. Their websites says some drivers can make $400 a month just by converting their car to an advert.

On the Immortality Bus, I'm trying to raise life extension issues—by provocatively telling people they don't want to end up in a coffin—so there's no money in it for me. But driving down the highway, it's easy to see how the future of advertising will change dramatically if it became cheap enough to send out autonomous vehicles to do capitalism's bidding.

****

14) I Tried Direct Neurofeedback and the Results Surprised Me

Transhumanism—the movement of using science and technology to improve the human being—covers many different fields of research. There are exoskeleton suits to help the disabled; there are stem cell treatments to cure disease; there are robots and AI to perform human chores. The field is wide open and booming as humanity uses more and more tech in its world.

It's not that often I get to participate directly in these radical technologies, but I did so recently when Grant Rudolph, clinical director at Echo Rock Neurotherapy in Mill Valley, California, invited me to try his direct neurofeedback techniques. Via his computer and EEG wire hookups, Rudolph echoed my brainwave information back into my head at an imperceptible level. I did two sessions of direct neurofeedback.

At first, I was skeptical that I'd even feel anything since the EEG information can't be detected by the skin as a sensation, but within five minutes of having the wires stuck onto my forehead, I began feeling different. I can compare it to a light dose of a recreational drug: I felt happy, content, and worry-free. I also felt more introspective than normal. The feedback only took a few seconds, and after about 15 minutes, I seemed to notice the world's colors were sharper and my hearing was more acute. The heightened awareness and calming effect lasted about 24 hours and then most of it gradually wore off. Some of the clarity must still be working, because getting things done sometimes still seems easier. I'm told that continued sessions would make this state of clarity my new norm.

I wanted to share my experience with my readers. Here's a short interview I conducted with Grant Rudolph to explain more about direct neurofeedback:

Q. What do most people notice from direct neurofeedback?

A. Direct neurofeedback (LENS) shows the brain how to stop worrying and be fully present in this moment. Victoria Vogel and I have given about 20,000 sessions at Echo Rock Neurotherapy, and the first words we hear clients say are usually "relaxed, calm or clear." The immediate experience for almost everyone is an unusual deep relaxation and simultaneous bright clarity of mind. When this state keeps going for days, they eventually talk about their new traits of steady happiness, increased energy, confidence, clear boundaries, better sleep, work efficiency, and ongoing contentment.

Q. How does it work?

A. Direct neurofeedback allows people to let go of stress by showing the survival brain how it is wasting energy worrying about the past. Because our brains are very interested in energy-efficiency, they quickly abandon unskillful defensive thought-patterns once they "see" them. Direct neurofeedback supplies the missing information. Unlike biofeedback and traditional neurofeedback where the "seeing" happens with the cognitive mind, direct neurofeedback information returns transcranially through the EEG sensor wires, bypassing the cognitive process altogether. Change is easy because the wise brain simply knows what to do and makes the adjustments without effort.

Q. What conditions does it treat?

A. Direct neurofeedback clears the underlying causes of stress rather than chasing after symptoms. Therefore it is safe and effective in addressing all sorts of conditions. It has shown itself clinically successful in treating depression and fatigue, anxiety, ADHD, memory loss, PTSD, learning disabilities & autism, procrastination, head trauma, migraines, addiction, pain and much more. It can be highly effective with treatment-resistant seizure disorders and compulsive behavior. For people without a diagnosis, it enhances performance, efficiency and meditation progress. We are offering a neurofeedback enhanced meditation retreat November 24-26 this year.

Q. Who does it work for?

A. Individuals of all ages can benefit from direct neurofeedback. At Echo Rock Neruotherapy, we help super-achievers—CEOs, Olympic athletes, musicians and the like—to find their flow state and achieve peak performance. Because it is so fast and easy to administer, direct neurofeedback has been extremely effective at treating children who are on the ADHD/autism spectrum, or have behavioral, learning or attachment problems, even if they are not actively participating in the treatment. For those struggling with relationship issues, direct neurofeedback can break old patterns, allowing the love between two people to bloom.

Q. What about medications and addictions?

A. As the brain becomes more spacious, organized, and better able to effectively utilize input, clients may find themselves less in need of medication. It is important, of course, to work with a medical professional like our in-house psychiatrist to taper down medications and determine the new ideal dosage.

Clients who struggle with addiction often feel so much better after a few sessions that it becomes easy to let go of their substance of choice. Withdrawal from opiates and even benzodiazepines can be considerably smoother with direct neurofeedback. When the brain is clear, clients typically find themselves naturally making wiser choices about how to best take care of themselves.

Q. How did you get started doing direct neurofeedback?

A. I was doing a practice of noticing situations where it was appropriate for me to say the words "I'm happy for you." At the same time, I wanted to help my son who had been failing at school because he fell and hit his head. He was irritable, and couldn't focus or sit still. We tried everything, until we finally gave him direct neurofeedback. For the first time in his life, he could read a book, and pass a test on what it said. Direct neurofeedback worked so dramatically, that we offered it to all our psychotherapy clients. They were able to resolve their issues easily and immediately, without talking about their past. Now we have the pleasure of helping people having a hard time with their headspace every day. After direct neurofeedback, they are relieved and grateful, and I get to say the words "I'm happy for you!"

****

CHAPTER III: POLITICS

15) A Transhumanist Goes to the Presidential Conventions

Somewhere between a roaming white llama, a purple face-painted dancing mystic, and a pack of born-again, sign-waving Christians screaming that I was going to burn in hell, I saw the irritated soul of America.

It wasn't the America you see on CNN or hear about on NPR, but rather it resembled a traveling circus performing under the sprawled-out tent of democracy—and the tent was faded and fraying at the edges.

Either way, as the 2016 Transhumanist Party Presidential candidate—someone who advocates for robot rights, brain implants, and AI to one day replace all government—I fit right in.

Earlier this month, my volunteers and I had decided to attend both 2016 national conventions—the GOP convention in Cleveland (which ended last week) and the Democratic Convention in Philadelphia (which ends Thursday). We wanted to be the voice of science and technology at these 50,000+ person gatherings. Political conventions are known for being wild affairs, but this year promised to be more so since both nominated candidates were historically disliked.

At first, I felt sheepish crashing another candidate's political coronation. Of course, I wasn't allowed inside the conventions—only speakers, delegates, journalists, and special guests are let in. But standing outside the Philadelphia Wells Fargo Convention Center and the Cleveland Quicken Loans Arena, amidst the thousands of protesters and activists that were there, I realized I was right at home. What I didn't suspect, though, was how different the conventions would be from one another.

Most people are still coming to terms with Donald Trump as the Republican nominee. A year ago, a convention dedicated to Trump seemed outlandish, but he managed to pull it off and score the nomination. Millions of Americans—not just Ted Cruz and Mitt Romney—are still in shock and utterly dismayed that a celebrity non-politician has the GOP crown.

Because of this, the feeling on the street in Cleveland was supposed to be one of grievance, despair and even possibly terror and violence. Gauging by the sheer amount of armed police on the ground in downtown Cleveland, you'd think it was a war zone. In the end, the convention went off pretty much without a hitch, and instead of chaos, many protesters like me found a posh street party, cute cafes, and even some celebration (presumably because no one was shot protesting). Like thousands of others, I surprisingly enjoyed myself.

That doesn't mean the Public Square wasn't tense. It was filled with Alex Jones and company yelling at communists. Anti-abortion and Black Lives Matter protests also occurred. Police had to form tight lines to keep the peace a few times. But the vibe was distinctly not dangerous or hostile. Trump winning the nomination somehow made us all look at ourselves, shake our heads, and chuckle. His win broadened our experience of America. People will say it's not in ways we want—but surely it's in ways that are true to who we are, for better or worse. People celebrated that, and even the often smiling police—who once arrested 400 people at a Republican convention in 2000, but arrested only 24 people this time—knew that.

On the other hand, the Democratic convention was solemn—even amidst various protests. Unlike the GOP convention, no one expected violence at the DNC—but no one also expected such sadness, too. Thousands of protesters were yelling and mourning over Bernie Sanders and the political revolution he started but couldn't finish. One woman told me tearfully she traveled 1,500 miles in hopes the Democratic delegates might somehow still make Sanders the nominee. On Monday, I watched glimmers of hope pass from hundreds of faces as Bernie promoted Hillary Clinton in his speech on the conference opening day. On Tuesday, as Hillary was historically championed the Democratic nominee, some people packed up and left Philly.

Amongst this scene, I tried campaigning and gaining new voters. Unfortunately, my techno-optimist message was difficult to hear. When I told protesters my goal was to get science and technology to play a more dominant role in American culture, many responded saying these were secondary issues—and currently unimportant. The Sanders fans wanted equality, college debt banished, and police brutality to stop. As soon as I told them I supported a Universal Basic Income, free education, and green tech to solve climate change, they took a liking to me. But science and technology, sadly, was not on their minds.

Another interesting point about the convention was protester diversity. For all the criticism that Trump and the Republican Party gets about being racist, the protesters (and supporters) outside the GOP convention were packed with diversity. There was an extremely large amount of different races, creeds, ethnicities, political philosophies, and social movements afoot—including an all women's group of "Muslims for science," which I appreciated. The protesters and supporters that couldn't get into the Democratic convention were nothing of the sort. Everywhere I looked were young, white Americans, many camping out at FDR Park in South Philly. Diversity was limited, even if everyone was preaching for it. On the other hand, regarding gender, I did see more women protesters at the DNC than the RNC.

Another major difference between the conventions was the interaction between delegates and the public. In Cleveland, I spoke to many delegates—the street leading to the entrance was not barricaded and open to the public. In Philadelphia, 8-foot-tall gates, sometimes-closed-off subway stations, and poor planning made it difficult to talk to any delegates—which ultimately resulted in distant angry protests against many of them (instead of potentially helpful 1-on-1 conversations). Many people commented on the irony of Hillary having more so-called "walls" up than Trump.

Interestingly, many of the delegates I spoke to at the GOP convention didn't seem to care what my futurist policies were or weren't. What they cared about was that the transhumanist ideas I suggested could move the economy forward. Luckily, they can, I insisted. Gene editing tech, exoskeleton technology, and driverless cars—core transhumanist issues—are going to make many new billionaires. The delegates smiled, welcoming me to the club, asking if GOP speaker and transhumanist Peter Thiel was a friend of mine.

This wasn't the way it was supposed to be. I tend to lean a bit left in my policies, and the Christian right—rulers of the GOP—were supposed to despise me. After all, I'm an atheist candidate. Yet, it turned out, at least at their convention, that my musings were welcome.

The Transhumanist Party and my campaign generally aim to be politically centric, and we focus on how we can best promote a science and technology agenda. Nothing on Planet Earth affects our lives more than innovation in science and tech, so you'd think the major candidates would be talking more about it. Sadly, they're not. It's politics as usual with them, which is perhaps why so many Americans are disgruntled about the major candidate choices they have.

I wasn't the only outsider presidential candidate to crash the conventions. Libertarian Gary Johnson visited the Republican Convention, and Jill Stein of the Green Party led rallies at the Democratic Convention. If the major parties aren't careful, and don't listen more to the demands of the American people, 2016 might be remembered as the year the two-party system disappeared. For me, that would be a welcome respite to the defeatist political circus America has become. New voices and ideas—and more than two major national conventions to protest and party at—might just be the new norm.

****

16) The Libertarian Futurist's Case for Avoiding War and Military Entanglements

Some of the early years of my adult life were in conflict zones as a journalist—which included covering the Pakistan/Indian Kashmir conflict for the National Geographic Channel and *The New York Times Syndicate*. War zones are terrifying. One always is worried about bullying soldiers, speeding armed military vehicles, stray bullets, and whether there's a roadside bomb on your path. Anyone that approaches you is suspect and could be carrying ready-to-detonate explosives.

One thing conflict zones teach you is that freedom is precious. The nearly 70-year Kashmir conflict has approximately a half million soldiers involved, so even if they're supposedly on your side (depending on what country you're in), you still feel under siege. My time in certain parts of Sudan, Israel, Palestine, Zimbabwe, Lebanon, Sri Lanka, Eritrea, Mali, and Yemen left me with the same feeling.

We face an unusual time with President Trump, whose bold behavior could prove dangerous to stable foreign policy. This situation has now become even more worrisome this month when Russia's Vladimir Putin, according to RT, said publicly that whoever "leads in artificial intelligence will rule the world." Some experts believe we will have an AI equivalent to human intelligence in less than 10 years time—which means in 15-20 years time, AI will far outdo human thinking and could be in control of all nuclear weaponry on the planet.

For this reason, nothing is more critical for nations and peoples to strive for peaceful times and to get along with one another. In any kind of modern conflict or 21st Century arms race—AI, genetic engineering, or nuclear arms—we likely will lose some of our freedoms and sense of security.

The implementation of the Patriot Act during George W. Bush's presidency was a good example of how we lost freedoms. Notably, libertarians hated it.

Furthermore, in heated times of conflict—as troublesome Kim Jong-un and North Korea seem bent on achieving—civilization also takes on far more serious existential risk. The world must always remember there are now 25,000 nuclear weapons on the planet. War is emotional and can get out of hand way too quickly for our own good, no matter who is right or wrong.

It's always best to lessen conflict and try to work things out. It's always better to attempt peaceful negotiations and compromise, rather than accept military intervention. This doesn't mean as a libertarian California 2018 gubernatorial candidate (and a possible 2020 libertarian presidential candidate) I wouldn't advocate for military fighting under certain circumstances, but if America and the world want to continue down a path of lasting prosperity, we must passionately avoid new and old foreign conflicts.

My novel *The Transhumanist Wager* recounts some of my experiences in a conflict zone:

Fourteen miles from Muzaffarabad, near the Line of Control in Pakistani Kashmir, a small bombed village is awash in activity—in tragedy. It's desperate and shocking. An old woman runs up to me, throwing her hands at my face. All ten of her fingers are pointing in unnatural directions—broken in different ways. She's another torture victim. To my right, a man wanders the dirt roads, calling out his child's name. In another part of the village, younger women grieve, complaining of multiple gang rapes by soldiers. I try to interview the husbands—those who are still alive refuse, turn away, and cry. War is a frothing beast.

People forget or don't realize it only takes a few hours for a political conflict between nations to escalate to a world war where tens of millions may die. It's happened before. We must use caution and balance to take us forward. We are at a very special point in history, when science, technology, and the field of transhumanism will soon allow many amazing possibilities for America and the human race—possibly ushering in the greatest era of prosperity humanity as a whole has ever known.

But so far, technology, science, and our own behavior have not given us the hope they will stop war. We must therefore be on our guard not to incite war—and we must not pick leaders that have a propensity to lead us into armed conflict. We must aim to remain bound by reason, compassion, and peacefulness at all times.

****

17) Is Monetizing Federal Land the Way to Pay for Basic Income?

Between now and the end of Donald Trump's first term in 2020, it's likely millions of jobs in America will be lost to automation, software and robots. Depending on how fast technology evolves, that human job-loss number might even rival that of the Great Recession of 2007, where more than eight million people were put out of work, and America's banking system nearly collapsed.

By 2030, the job losses will likely be in the tens of millions. McDonald's will flip burgers with machines, Amazon will deliver packages with drones and taxis will all be self-driving. Even white-collars jobs, like those on Wall Street, will be replaced by artificial intelligence — the world's largest hedge fund has already set plans in motion for this.

Like the Titanic, capitalism is sinking, but few passengers are wondering yet if there are enough lifeboats.

I recently declared my run as a Libertarian for California governor in 2018, and I gently support the idea of a state-funded basic income to offset the effects of ubiquitous automation. A basic income would give every Californian some money — and it makes sense to start such a dramatic program here in the Golden State, since this is where much of the human-job-replacing-tech is created.

My Libertarian friends are skeptical of my support for a basic income. They insist the only way to pay for such a program is via higher taxes. This is not true; other ways exist. California could potentially cut deals with the federal government to lease its empty land and natural resources to help pay for a basic income.

After all, state and federal resources belong to the people, and 45 percent of California (more than 45 million acres) is government-controlled land, leaving vast areas idle and mostly undeveloped.

Environmentalists go bonkers at this idea, but they fail to understand modern science and how fast it's evolving. Take for example: wood — one of the most commonly used natural resources in the world.

Everything from homes to furniture to Starbucks coffee cups are made from it. But that's unlikely to continue. In 20 years' time or less, dozens of stronger materials are likely to be constructed in laboratories that require far less money to mass produce than it takes to grow and harvest timber — in fact, various companies are already working on this right now. Using forests for building materials is way too laborious to survive in the 21st century.

And even if it did, it would only be because genetic engineering and nanotechnology would allow us to grow trees at many times the current natural rate — something scientists are also already tinkering with.

The story of the timber industry's future is not unique. Other major Californian natural resource businesses — such as fossil fuels, agriculture and fisheries — will suffer the same extinction or complete technological transformation of its industry.

The world is changing. Nature will no longer be what the Earth gives us, but what we create of Earth with our radical new tools.

Despite opposition by environmentalists and Luddites, we should consider focusing more on humanitarian possibilities from use of California's natural resources. We can do that by distributing those resources directly back to the people — in a monthly monetary form the average citizen can use for healthcare, food and opportunity.

The Federal government's net worth of natural resources is at least $130 trillion dollars. California is the third largest state in the U.S., and its 45 million federal acres of land could be worth $10 to $20 trillion dollars.

As a potential governor, I wouldn't advocate for actually selling off California — nor destroying its natural beauty — but rather leasing it out. This would mean that the bulk of land and natural resources — as well as its value — always remain California's in the long run. This type of deal would be easy to administer; there are endless businesses and ventures out there that will gladly pay the people to make something of idle lands and untapped wealth.

It's also true that some limited amount of federal land in California is already leased out for profit by the Bureau of Land Management (BLM) and U.S. Forest Service (USFS).

Along with California's state and national park tourism, as well as other wilderness and recreational areas that charge fees, these endeavors make good money. But you and I, as tax-paying residents, don't really feel it or know about it — and we certainly don't get a paycheck for it. I'd rather California be like Alaska, where everybody every year gets cut a state check.

And how much money would Californians receive every year from its natural resources, assuming we use its midpoint valuation of $15 trillion dollars? It turns out, quite a bit, if at least 75 percent of the state's federal land was leased out and it provided a 5 percent return, which is pretty standard.

If every household — and there are about 13 million in California — received this sort of 5 percent annual payout, it would be about $57,500 per household, or nearly $5,000 a month. In short, it would dramatically change the lives of tens of millions of people — especially the nearly 40 percent of Californians who live at, below or near the poverty line of $24,000 for a family of four.

Surprisingly, by utilizing California's land and natural resources, it would be more than enough to create a permanent livable basic income for everyone in the state — in fact, there would be so much money in the state coffers that we could dramatically cut taxes, too. California wouldn't need to worry about its poor, about Medi-Cal or about low-income housing again. Right now, California has some of the highest taxes of any U.S. state, but that could all change as the state's poor would instantly receive middle-class incomes. Entire government aid agencies could be shut down.

Naysayers will beat their chests about this plan, citing all the reasons it could never happen. But like it or not, in the future, a basic income must happen. The alternative is downright dystopian, since the issue with robots taking everyone's jobs will inevitably lead to a dangerous climax: revolution, or no revolution.

For example, if driverless trucks take away the 3.5 million human trucking jobs in America (which is on track to start happening in the next three to five years), what will those truckers do? Many of them will not be able to get other jobs or be retrained, because robots will soon take those jobs they trained for.

The thing to know about truckers — and I personally met quite a few of them during my cross-country Transhumanist 2016 presidential campaign bus tour — is that most of them are proud, gun-bearing tough guys — the kind you want at your side when a fight breaks out in a bar. It would be wise to offer them a livable income in return for the robots taking away their livelihoods — otherwise, there's a real chance they'll revolt and cause much civil strife.

Naturally, the same will happen when you take away the other tens of millions of jobs inevitably to be replaced by 2030.

We should all remember it's not like this dilemma of government transference is brand new either — it just happens to be kept mostly quiet.

Nearly half of Americans already receive some sort of government assistance to live on — quite possibly, so they don't revolt, whether at the voting booth or by civil disobedience. This support includes welfare, food stamps, Medicaid, social security and myriad other programs. And the brunt of it is borne on the taxes we pay.

One of the core principles of Libertarianism is the non-aggression principle — the idea that unprovoked aggression against a person or their property is morally wrong. The thorny 21st century question for all Libertarians is: Does technology — specifically automation that takes away livelihood — qualify as immoral aggression against people?

While the classic Libertarian philosophy would say that a free market place is the best one, and I do believe this is true economically, such ideology is too tough to swallow for the tens of millions of workers who are slowly realizing machines will soon make competition all but impossible for them. Our entire economic system will need to change, or it will lead to riots, an overwhelming homeless population and huge swaths of Americans that go hungry. It will also lead to extreme inequality, a major factor for why wars start.

Before going any further, it's important to note that basic income isn't entirely new for Libertarians. In the past, a number of Libertarian thinkers, like Milton Friedman and Charles Murray, have supported forms of basic income, praising the fact it would inevitably swallow the plethora of government aid programs.

The savings by this massive government consolidation into a single payer payout could save hundreds of billions of dollars by eliminating administrative costs and wasteful bureaucracy.

Some of my friends will say as a Libertarian I lean too left, and my support of a basic income is too government-oriented. But I think it presents an incredible opportunity for Libertarianism to grow into a bona fide leadership role on the national political stage — especially if it can do so with tax-free-emphasizing alternatives, like leasing out federal land.

I think the Libertarian Party could be the first major political party to embrace the new economic order — and gain prominence by it.

Nicholas Sarwark, chair of the Libertarian Party, recently said in a moving speech at the Southern California Conference: the Libertarian Party is the party of love of people.

I agree with him. We love the rights of our neighbors and ourselves, and we will protect them.

However, when no one can compete against machines because our own inventiveness has outdone us — and the great majority of us have no way to survive — we must step in to love ourselves and our neighbors enough to protect our essential ability to exist.

A basic income is about national and state ownership rights of all citizens and the free market creating a birthright paycheck that protects us all in the machine age, and I believe it's in direct support of a broad interpretation of the libertarian non-aggression principle. It's about returning our country's resources directly to the people so we can all thrive — and no person or machine can steal our wealth or fundamental livelihood.

Despite what many conservatives or liberals think, Libertarianism is not an economic system, but a social philosophy based on protecting rights of the individual. Government is not the enemy or the savior of the people. Government is just a mirror of our united selves, through which we can transfer the resources of the people to the people. In the machine age, that allocation would best begin with a basic income, facilitated by fully monetizing our country's natural resources for citizens to financially utilize.

****

18) Why I'm Not Taking Any Contributions for my Presidential Run

Like many Americans, I was taught from an early age that any natural-born citizen 35 years or older can become president. I've always relished that supposed fact. It meant that regardless of class, gender, education, ethnicity, and wealth, one could aspire to what is arguably the world's most important and powerful position.

Unfortunately, it was a lie. What they forgot to mention was that you needed money to win the presidency— hundreds of millions of dollars. Naively, I didn't discover this until I actually began my 2016 presidential run.

Early into my campaign, I became disillusioned with my ability to run for the Presidency. Without the sponsorship of a billionaire funding me (or the ability to raise many millions of dollars), there was basically no chance to be competitive. So I made the difficult choice to not accept campaign funds or donations at all—both as a form of protest and a means of honesty.

In 2014, I declared my candidacy for the Transhumanist Party, a smallish political entity that endorses transhumanism—a social movement that aims to use science and technology to radically improve humanity. For my presidential campaign, I had planned to raise funds and follow the Federal Election Commission (FEC) rules closely. I even visited the FEC office in Washington DC to make sure I understood everything. Sadly, understanding it is like understanding the US tax code—a near impossibility.

The finance rule books I was given by an FEC staff member were overwhelming, not dissimilar from the FEC's daunting 198 page Congressional Candidates and Committees book presidential candidates also use. As a former journalist for National Geographic and a philosophy major, I consider myself pretty well-equipped to deal with the English language. But nothing could prepare me for the byzantine presidential accounting laws.

In the first day of my campaign, I accidentally broke various rules. The finance laws were written for mainstream candidates, not lesser known candidates running smaller campaigns. There are hundreds of us in the 2016 race.

For independents seeking the Presidency, it's essentially only possible to run as symbolic candidate. The most you can reasonably accomplish is to get public and media attention for your cause and at best a fraction of America's vote.

Even getting your name on state ballots as a candidate is a herculean task, reserved only for the resources of the super rich. Every state has different requirements and convoluted guidebooks. Some states—mostly the important ones—require huge amounts of signatures and fees.

The donation link on my website is crossed out in red, and leads to a page with a short explanation. I've been paying for my campaign all out of my pocket. The one exception is my Immortality Bus, which I crowdfunded over 45 days for just over $27,000 and use to promote transhumanism (and, on occasion, my campaign).

Crowdfunding is not technically allowed in presidential campaigns. At the same time, special interest groups, lobbyists, and Super PACs dominate elections, funneling tens of millions of dollars to influence the public so their candidate wins. In 2010, US court rulings summed up as Citizens United upped the ante by allowing Political Action Committees to spend unlimited on their candidates, so long as their candidates aren't involved. For example, in 2012, the Super PAC supporting Mitt Romney called Restore our Future took in nearly $100 million dollars.

My candidacy is being run on less than $100,000—a drop in the bucket compared the bigger names. So what can independents do?

We could follow some of the basic rules that Lawrence Lessig tried to put forth in his short presidential campaign. His ideas go like this (taken from his website):

All citizens deserve equal access to the ballot.

The Citizen Equality Act will guarantee the equal freedom to vote by passing the Voting Rights Advancement Act of 2015 and the Voter Empowerment Act of 2015. In addition, we will enact automatic voter registration and turn election day into a national holiday.

All citizens deserve equal representation in Congress.

The Citizen Equality Act will give each voter as close to equal political influence as possible by redrawing districts and restructuring election systems. It will use FairVote's "Ranked Choice Voting Act" to end political gerrymandering and create multi-member districts with ranked-choice voting for Congress.

All citizens deserve an equal ability to choose our leaders.

The Citizen Equality Act will end pay-to-play politics by changing the way we fund campaigns by taking the best of Rep. Sarbanes' Government by the People Act, and Represent US's "American Anti-Corruption Act." That hybrid would give every voter a voucher to contribute to fund congressional and presidential campaigns; it would provide matching funds for small-dollar contributions to congressional and presidential campaigns. And it would add effective new limits to restrict the revolving door between government service and work as a lobbyist.

Adding to this, I'd suggest a system that disallows Super PACs entirely, unless there's a method to ensure independents can also successfully be included in the system.

Changing the system of how we vote for a President could be an important moment in history for the American people. No other job on this planet requires such a steadfast commitment of a free and unbiased system to be chosen. And someone's ban account should not decide whether they are considered for the world's most important job.

The worst thing I can say about the presidential process right now is perhaps also the one that pains me the most as a patriot: Our presidential election process is incredibly un-American.

****

19) To Grow 3rd Party Politics in America, Make John McAfee the Libertarian Party Nominee (Updated Version)

From the author Zoltan Istvan (4/14/2016): A change of opinion about John McAfee has made me retract my endorsement of him as the best Libertarian Party presidential nominee in the 2016 election. I still like John McAfee and believe he is an excellent promoter of freedom, but no longer the best candidate for growing Third-Party politics or the Libertarian Party in America.

In America and around the world, people are in disbelief over the 2016 US Presidential election so far. Bernie Sanders has risen to become a legend for the youth and hard left leaning. Trump is on his way to forever transforming the Republican Party and likely challenging Hillary Clinton for the most powerful position in the world. Cruz and Rubio, like tens of millions of Americans, are standing baffled at what has transpired in the last year.

The elections have become a flamboyant game show. And the people in the audience cheering the most are shareholders of media companies who are selling more ads than ever.

Unfortunately, much of the chaos and media antics haven't translated too favorably yet for Third parties. Quietly, candidates like myself at the Transhumanist Party, attempt to spread our messages. Don't get me wrong. We are succeeding, but not in the way that America deserves. America owes it to itself to hear the plight of the other leading 50 presidential candidates out there, who also bear important messages. Many of them are astute people that would likely govern well, like Harvard educated physician Jill Stein of the Green Party and Rod Silva of the Nutrition Party.

The good news for America is that the Libertarian Party will probably be on all 50 state ballots, meaning it's possible that the Libertarian Party presidential candidate could significantly alter the outcome of the elections.

This could especially be the case if a colorful enough character is the nominee for the Libertarian Party. It's possible the Libertarian candidate could get enough votes to sway the election one way of the other—or at least the media might play it that way for the six months leading up to the elections.

Controversial, volatile, and having more fun than the other candidates, John McAfee could be just the Libertarian candidate America needs to further continue the positive change Trump and Sanders have caused to America's stale political infrastructure. McAfee might have a checkered past, but that's not what's important. What's important is he has charisma and is very media savvy. Like Trump, you can't tear him down, because McAfee thrives off chaos and controversial press coverage. I met McAfee and his friendly wife recently in North Carolina on my presidential campaign bus tour. I debated McAfee, laughed with him, and even drank Scotch with him. I'm quite sure of what I'm writing here.

If McAfee is the Libertarian nominee, he has the ability to do to Third-Party politics what Trump has done to this election cycle. McAfee can elevate the Libertarian Party so that major media is forced to cover it again and again and again. Now that would be something—and it would help the plight of all independent candidates and other Third parties.

Additionally, at least McAfee is talking technology, cybersecurity, and transhumanism, something none of the other candidates seem to even think is important—even though nothing affects human beings and society as much as these advancing fields.

Even though I like many of the other Libertarian presidential candidates, I recommend McAfee as a tech celebrity to gain the Libertarian nomination when it is decided. McAfee is capable of gaining consistent widespread attention in the political national conversation, and thereby putting the major parties on alert that Third-Party politics is something to be reckoned with. Done right, McAfee might even be able to get frontrunners of the Republican and Democratic parties to publicly embrace select Libertarian values to capture additional votes in 2016. I often publicly identify as a left-leaning Libertarian, so I know this would be great for the Libertarian Party to get its message out there.

Personally, I despise the Two-Party system in our country. It's completely un-American, and is just another form of monopoly—except with two heads ruling instead of one. To help fight it, we should embrace explosive personalities who can destroy a political system that favors big money and special interests—neither of which Sanders, Trump, or McAfee need or are beholden to.

Come November, the race will likely come down to Trump and Clinton, but the real winner might be the growing Libertarian Party—and by implication, other Third parties—by putting forth a loud personality who can get America cheering in a very different way. That is progress, indeed.

****

20) Gary Johnson Wants Driverless Secret Service Cars and a US-Led Gene Editing Revolution

I recently sat down with Libertarian Presidential candidate Gary Johnson at his home in New Mexico and watched an episode of Orphan Black, the hit sci-fi show. Between his CNN Town Hall meetings and endless speeches on the campaign trail, you're probably asking: How did Gary get the time to watch a television show? It's a good question, but the former Governor made the time, because he's interested in the future and willing to explore how it might unfold.

Johnson is excited about using radical science and technology to make America stronger and help the human race.

Nothing else will change America more in the coming decades than radical science and technology. Consider CRISPR gene editing tech and the biohackers who are already trying to splice plant DNA in their skin to be able to photosynthesize energy into their bodies. Talk about a way to end world hunger. Or what about artificial intelligence and nuclear weapons—something Bill Gates and Stephen Hawking have recently publicly worried about? Some experts believe coming AI—an intelligence as smart as an adult human being—could arrive in as little as a decade with enough funding.

Gary Johnson is interested in these things and has ideas about them.

I had the pleasure of talking about it with him while he cooked me dinner and had me as an overnight guest in home (he makes a mean shrimp and scallop pasta). My visit was predicated upon being a possible Vice Presidential choice of his. Given the remarkable personalities also on Johnson's radar (like Governor Bill Weld who he chose), I probably was a long shot for the position. But that didn't stop Johnson from spending

2 half-days with me discussing radical technology and the best way to use it to improve America.

PREPARING AMERICA FOR A NEW AGE IN SCIENCE AND TECHNOLOGY

When Johnson talks about improving America, he really means it. In fact, I believe it's the main reason he's running for the US presidency. He worries about America imminently having a cultural and financial meltdown that could irreparably harm this nation—and the world with it. Johnson asserts that he wants to restore commonsense social open-mindedness and fiscal responsibility to our nation before that happens.

It's not going to be easy for Johnson.

As a well-known extreme athlete and sports competitor, he's in for the race of his life. He's likely to be on all 50 state ballots and technically could win the Presidency, but that's only probable if he's included in the national debates with Trump and Clinton. To be included he has to reach 15% consistently in the polls. He's in the low double digits now, but improving every month.

I strongly believe Gary Johnson should be in the debates, whether he makes the arbitrary 15% threshold or not. I believe this not only because it breaks up America's monopolistic and un-American two-party system, but because Johnson brings a unique perspective to politics with his forward-thinking about science, technology, and future.

ON THE ISSUES

I recently consulted with the US Navy on all things transhuman—including the development of AI. The four naval officers that came to my house in San Francisco were well aware of how important and disruptive this field will be. In an email, I asked Johnson what he thought of those that want to regulate AI, and he wrote, "I think it is important to not regulate the AI industry." Johnson said the same thing about the internet industry. As a Libertarian, he wants to leave those industries to themselves. Not regulating AI development goes against some leading thinkers like Elon Musk, but it's right in line with many AI engineers who argue there's little reason to worry about its creation.

Johnson also believes in longevity research. He says he would "sign legislation promoting research and development" of cures for all diseases. In fact, he likes the Facebook's Mark Zuckerberg recent statements that we should aim to cure every disease before this century is out. Johnson also said he would be "vetoing legislation that would restrict" science development.

Johnson also isn't afraid to discuss another hot button topic: gene editing. Early in 2015, Chinese scientists used gene editing techniques on the first human embryo. Some scientists immediately sought a moratorium on the radical technology. However, today scientists generally seem to have mellowed out and experiments are proceeding. Many countries are moving forward with research, including the USA (where a federal and bioethics panel recently approved human trials).

I recently told a CNN Courageous produced panel I was on in New York City that CRISPR/Cas9—where DNA is manipulated in genes to get specific outcomes—is probably the most important 21st Century scientific breakthrough and could help eliminate most disease and physical ailments. Already, gene editing has cured some cancer, improved animal's physical muscles and bodies, and removed malaria from mosquitoes. But America has been hesitant to take the lead with this research, leaving China as the nation who might end up with the most patents and expertise. When asked about this, Johnson wrote me, "Yes, I think America should take the lead."

Like it or not, if America doesn't lead here, another nation will. And because other nations may be interested in augmenting their children's intelligence using gene editing tech, America must be vigilant that this doesn't lead to an entire generation that is literally biologically smarter than Americans.

Additionally, the economic ramifications of Johnson's perspective are huge. Many new billion dollar companies likely will be created around gene editing tech. Like the other great technology of the last 30 years—the internet—we want those companies to be US companies.

On a more fun note, Johnson told me he'd "absolutely" use a driverless secret service car. He's not afraid of having a robot drive the President around. Such a vehicle will surely be here before the end of the next President's term.

Johnson also told me he'd have a 3D printer put into the White House. It's been years since America got a new household appliance, and the 3D printing revolution happening right now might mean much less shopping at WalMart—and more making of things right in your home. I expect 3D printers to be in millions of homes within the next 10 years. My neighbor already has one.

The fact is this radical science and technology stuff is not only super cool, but incredibly important. America is entering an age when discussion of immigration, social security, and foreign defense may not be as important as artificial intelligence, gene editing tech, and curing all diseases. Gary Johnson is a candidate willing to address these hot-button issues.

I hope Johnson will make it into the Presidential debates (and Bill Weld into the Vice Presidential debates), so along with his fiscal and social policies, he'll be able to share with America a brave vision on the future. Gary Johnson is a top-notch presidential candidate for American science and technology for two reasons: He's excited about it—and he's willing to openly talk about the issues.

****

21) I Went to the Largest Freedom Festival in the World and Here's What I Saw

Last month, I attended FreedomFest, the largest festival in the world dedicated to free minds and liberty. Spanning four days in Las Vegas, it was the event's 10th anniversary, and thousands of fans attended. A line-up of celebrity speakers like William Shatner, Steve Forbes, and John Stossel gave the festival media power and Hollywood glam. The hundreds of booths dedicated to guns, Bitcoin, and Ayn Rand clubs completed the spectacle.

I went to the event expecting to see anarchists, tea partiers, and libertarians attending talks with automatic weapons strung across their shoulders, but the gilded, chandelier-laden Paris hotel where the festival was at didn't allow an armed public. German Shepherds and a number of police roamed the venue to make sure the rules were followed.

In fact, to my delight, the festival was steeped in intellectualism—a place where freedom-minded folk came to exchange ideas and policies, many of them about how to best preserve liberty in the challenging Trump-era. While plenty of Trump supporters did attend the festival (Trump himself spoke at FreedomFest in 2015) and a few conservative radio hosts broadcasted from their booths, my take away was that most festival goers associated the new US President with a lingering worry about fascism. In fact, one of the most attended and passionate forums was a main stage debate on whether Trump was good for American liberty.

This year's anniversary festival was themed "Exploring New Frontiers," and transhumanism and artificial intelligence was a topic on many attendee's minds. A half dozen well-attended panels—two of which I was on—were based on how radical science and technology are upending the species.

My first panel, called Artificial Intelligence and Robots: Economy of the Future or End of Free Markets? was created and opened by Heartland Institute Research Director Edward Hudgins. Michael Shermer, *New York Times* bestselling author and founding publisher of *Skeptic Magazine*, moderated the panel. Peter Voss, an AI scientist introduced how machine intelligence works, and how far it's come. Later I spoke on my Federal Land Dividend "basic income" plan to help support people who lose their jobs to robots—something I think will happen rapidly to most workers within 25 years. Gennady Stolyarov, Chairman of the Transhumanist Party spoke on the future rights of robots. Futurist Eric Shuss spoke on using AI to improve America's education system.

Based on the main raised eyebrows and questions of the audience, it seemed most people were unaware how fast automation and AI was coming. Some experts believe we could have a machine intelligence as smart as humans on planet Earth in 10-15 years time if enough money is put into the field. Other experts, like Voss believe that's too soon—and he was quick to point out that human intelligence and our three-pound brains are far more complex than many futurists or engineers like to admit.

Near the end of our AI panel, one visibly upset man from the audience asked why none of us spoke of the abomination of giving AI human attributes. He was clearly alluding to a fundamental religious position. Since nearly everyone on the panel was pro-transhumanism and pro-AI, this was a rhetorical question for us, though not unwarranted given that 75 percent of Americans identify as Christians. Stolyarov answered saying attempts would be made to protect the rights of AI and intelligent beings, but this angry man clearly believed that robots should not ever be made smarter than their maker.

My next panel was part of Reason Day, put on by *Reason Magazine*. Called Liberating the Human Body, I joined veteran science writer Ronald Bailey, *Reason* editor-at-large Matt

Welch, and distinguished professor Dierdre McCloskey, who famously transitioned from a man to a woman at age 53. We each spoke for five minutes about our transhumanist perspectives of modifying the human body.

Bailey spent most of his talk discussing genetic editing, and how revolutionary the new science is. Most libertarian and free-minded people want the government to stay entirely out of science, including gene editing. However, the coming (and in some cases current) ability to enhance one's IQ and body are thorny questions of society—since if only the rich can afford the technology, what's to keep classes of people from widening even further. And it's not only people. Genetic editing gives us the ability to possibly even merge species together. It's possible in a decade's time, people could be born with horns, extra functional limbs, and even with both male and female reproductive parts in the same body.

I support the science to do this, as well as the individual's rights to use this technology. But many in the audience—most who appeared over the age of 50—seemed to be shaking their heads in dismay at such a brave new world.

Later I attended other talks and panels, and my favorite was Is Spock Libertarian? The Politics of Science Fiction. Nick Gillespie, Editor-in-Chief of *Reason.com* and Reason TV, moderated the panel, which included Hugo-winning author David Brin, *Reason* Features Editor Peter Suderman, and Editor-in-Chief of *Reason Magazine,* Katherine Mangu-Ward. It was never really decided whether Star Trek's Spock was libertarian, but the fascinating conversation covered the history of science fiction and touched on the future might hold for the art form.

In between panels, I wandered the festival floor was, which was about the size of a football field and often crowded with people. In the middle of it was the bookstore, where bestselling authors like controversial American commentator Dinesh D'Souza hung out and interviewed with C-SPAN Book TV. One surprising thing for me on the festival floor was the amount of booths dedicated to ways to invest in gold. The booths I liked best were the ones dedicated to legalizing drugs—something I strongly support. I subscribed to their mailing lists and signed their petitions.

Also working the floor and trying to drum up donations were a number of libertarian political candidates, such as New York gubernatorial candidate Larry Sharpe, and California's City of Calimesa Mayor Jeff Hewitt, who is running for California's 42nd Assembly District. Some 2018 political campaigns for libertarians are already in full swing, and the Libertarian Party's goal next year is to get a record 2000 candidates running in the mid-term US elections.

In the evening, I wandered into the packed main stage auditorium. William Shatner, captain of the Star Trek spaceship USS Enterprise was doing his keynote live interview with economist Mark Skouson. A thousand people were listening carefully as the star with more than two million twitter followers told of life on *Star Trek*, often seen as an example of near-perfect free-minded future.

In his final question, Shatner was asked: What is the most important lesson in life? The crowd thought he was going to answer to have freedom. Instead, Shatner replied to have love.

******

22) Another Wild Week in my Transhumanism Campaign

The last week has been a whirlwind—and I think busiest of my 2-year presidential campaign. To begin with, I flew down to Los Angeles to be with Dave Rubin on the popular *Rubin Report*. Unbeknownst to me, Rubin is a big science fiction fan, which always means the interviews go great. Science fiction and transhumanism have been embedded together for decades. It's only in the last several years that transhumanism—via mind-reading headsets, exoskeleton suits, chip implants, and other tech—has really crossed from fiction into everyday life.

After returning to San Francisco, that Wednesday I went to RoboBusiness to speak. The stage was set near the conference floor, and there was a nice-sized crowd to hear my talk and see my slideshow. A week before the event, I wrote an article on the subject I spoke about—the coming of personal robot bodyguards—and the story was widely read in *VentureBeat*. After my talk, *The San Francisco Chronicle* did a great piece with fun pictures of the event. Journalist Benny Evangelista included a bit about my speech. My two favorite exhibitions on the conference floor were the robot-riding motorcycle and the 4-foot tall child-like robot helper (see lead photo).

The following day I woke at 4:45 AM and drove into San Francisco to do a radio broadcast at the *KQED* studio. I had been invited to be on a BBC World Service panel with Professor Lawrence Lessig, Greg Orman, Professor Marjorie Hershey, and host Owen Bennet Jones. Jill Stein also appeared on the show. The discussion centered on how 3rd parties might make more of a difference in American politics. I had a great time talking with some of these political heavyweights, and I broadly support Lessig's plan for campaign finance reform, which is one of the reasons I don't accept campaign finance donations. Most of us on the panel—including myself—agreed that Jill Stein and especially Gary Johnson should be included in the presidential debates with Clinton and Trump. You can find the discussion on the BBC.

Later that day, I left to fly to Florida, a state where I'm a Write-In candidate and have my 31 Electors lined up. I gave a workshop and public speech on transhumanism at the University of Central Florida. There was about a 100-person crowd for the speech—mostly students. CBC was on hand to film it and there was a lively Q & A after.

The most difficult question I answered was my last. It was on the environment. As I've written before, I believe in human-made climate change, but I don't believe the best way to fix that is by reducing humanity's carbon footprint. The best way to help the Earth is to fix it with radical new technologies. We can use CRISPR gene editing to learn to regrow rainforests 10 times faster. We can use nanotechnology to clean rivers. We can use cloning methods to replenish fish populations. Transhumanism can best save the Earth.

Some in the crowd of students at UCF were not pleased with these answers, but I find them far more likely to make a difference in the long term than the Paris Climate Change Agreement.

The next day I had the luck to be on my way to The Venus Project run by 100-year-old futurist Jacque Fresco and his partner Roxanne Meadows. I had a great time discussing the possibility of a Resource-Based Economy, but that will have to wait until another article, as there's much to discuss and contemplate. However, I had an amazing time and spent a wonderful night on the research property.

****

23) I Want My Felonies Back

I was never a drug dealer in the hyped-Hollywood type of way. I was just an 18-year-old kid spending a college semester in Idaho for the snowboarding opportunities. While there, a girlfriend got me a small bag of marijuana for smoking—less than an ounce—and on occasion I shared a baggie of an eighth with a friend and accepted some "thank you" money when offered. When two college freshmen contacted me and asked if they could get $80 dollars worth of pot from me, I thought little of it. I didn't know the guys personally, but I'd seen their faces around campus and my dorm. They seemed friendly enough, and, after all, it was just weed. What could go wrong?

A time was set to meet at a nearby parking lot, and soon the exchange was done. However, when I drove back to my dorm room, five undercover cars with flashing lights on their dashboards came out of nowhere and surrounded me. The cops stopped traffic on the road, drew their guns, pulled me out of my truck, slammed me again the hood, cuffed me, and drove me off to the police station.

Later I discovered the buyers were students in the college's criminal justice department—and they had been wired, recording everything I said to them. An interrogation officer told me it was the student cop's first sting operation. They must be so proud.

I was convicted of two felonies: distribution and possession of a narcotic substance. My sentence was two years prison time. However, as a first time offender, the judge let me shorten my sentence to 12 months of probation if I did 30 days in the county jail. I did the jail time so I could get the hell out of Idaho as soon as possible.

The reason I'm telling you this story is because of outrage—outrage at the United States government and the old conservative WASP men that still mostly run it. It's important to understand that becoming a felon, even for a minor non-violent crime, is no small issue when you're 18 years old. In addition to taking away various voting and gun rights, and being forced to submit to random drug tests, a felony makes it extremely difficult to ever get a normal job. It also costs a lot of money to go through the judicial system, and a felony is a serious derogatory social badge to most people in society. It's one that has cost me important relationships with girlfriends, friendships, and professional opportunities—all because of the harmless sale of the equivalent of a couple joints.

People often ask me why I advocate for complete legalization of all drugs. I have a simple answer: Because the government does not know what's best for me or others. From slavery to prohibition to women's voting rights to gay marriage to banning federal funding for stem cells, the one thing the American government has shown is how inept, ham-fisted, and backwards it can be.

I also advocate for legalization of drugs because a major European country, Portugal, is now over a decade into its experiment with a full legalization policy, and studies show their society's drug issues have statistically improved. Instead of spending a trillion dollars on the ineffective War on Drugs like the US has, Portugal has spent its resources on rehabilitation and educational programs for hard drug users, while leaving recreational drugs users to make their own decisions about what they put in their bodies.

My wife tells me I should feel a certain consolation that since the time of my drug bust in 1992, America has been slowly withdrawing from its conservative anti-drug fervor. Currently, 28 states broadly allow medical marijuana use, and eight states—Colorado, Washington, California, Alaska, Nevada, Maine, Oregon, and Massachusetts—now have made recreational use legal. Eventually, pot will likely become legal everywhere, including selling $80 worth to college students. It's a good thing, too. Less people will die from drunk driving (since weed will replace alcohol as the drug of choice, and pot is generally considered safer to drive under). And culture could use a legal natural drug that stretches our mind while giving us a good time. So all seems well, right? Wrong.

Wrong because myself and millions of other minor drug offenders are left holding the bag. It wasn't just a criminal sentence many of us received: The government permanently confiscated my Jeep Comanche and beloved Honda motorcycle during my bust. It also took what little cash I had and made me spend it on lawyers, judicial filings, and the convoluted court system. The total financial loss to me 25 years ago was about $20,000 dollars. If I had been able to invest that money, for example in the Dow Jones industrial stock market index, I'd have over $100,000 now. Even at straight inflation, I'd have nearly $40,000. The ACLU reports that 8.2 million people in America were arrested between 2001 and 2010 for marijuana offenses. *The Washington Post* says at least 137,000 are sitting in US jails on any given day of the week. Where is our compensation, now that the country is on its glacial way to legalizing pot and taxing the sale of it like it does beer?

My biggest regret is this: Under pressure to get a corporate job 10 years after the incident, and knowing I eventually wanted to end up in politics, I cowardly filed to have my felonies expunged and sealed in court—so employers and the public couldn't see the crimes. I willingly took this beautiful badge of moral and legal defiance against a foolhardy government and handed it back to them, asking them to hide it.

No more. I've recognized my errors. It's my turn to fight back. And I'm doing just that now just with my Libertarian run for California Governor, promoting both my past and pro-drug policies. Thousands of drug offenders and I want our felonies front and center. We don't want the government's inevitable habeas corpus when they likely make pot legal across the land over the next decade. We want to share—maybe even brag about—our drug adventures to our friends, neighbors, and supporters. And we also want compensation for the financial harm caused to us. We want a multi-billion dollar class action lawsuit that offers adequate reparation, perhaps in the form of tax write-offs, so as not to harm the American tax payer further over the drug war. As a gubernatorial candidate, I will push for reparation to become law.

However, money won't solve this all, at least not for me. The government unfairly harmed me and made me own my so-called crime, and now I righteously want it forever. I had to forge my persona, philosophies, and life around my felonies, at great teenage angst and much difficult learning. Now I aim to use all those lessons to further disobey unreasonable authority, to reduce the power of the state, and to be a proud disrupter of traditionalism. The government was wrong to arrest me 25 years ago when I drove into that parking lot and sold a tiny amount of drugs. Now I'm not going to let them forget it.

****

24) Should We Also Have A Small Private Market for the Coronavirus Vaccine?

I recently took *The New York Times* "Find your Place" in the vaccine line report, and I was near the bottom 10% timeline for getting the coronavirus vaccine. This means I'll be nearly last in getting the potentially lifesaving vaccine.

This upsets me since as a successful 47-year-old San Francisco business person, I pay a lot of taxes, and frankly, the government-sponsored creation and distribution of the vaccine rests mostly on high taxpayers such as myself—not the homeless or prison population which are far ahead of me in line. My sense of fairness and justice are being violated. Never before in my life have I felt so deeply: Who is John Galt?

Surely, there are thousands of other people who also think the vaccine distribution timeline is unacceptable of our government and our society. Why should the most productive of society—the people who everyone else financially relies on during times of crisis—be relegated to the back of the line when their lives are also at stake?

My wife is a physician, and she disagrees with me. She says the strategy of who gets the vaccine first is based on saving the most amount of lives while protecting the most vulnerable. She insists the rich can afford good healthcare to fight coronavirus and can successfully hunker down in their comfortable homes to keep safe until vaccinated. The unhealthy, the homeless, and the essential worker making minimum wage cannot.

These are good arguments, which nearly all people agree with. But it doesn't satisfy the sense of fairness in my philosophical mind—and how much financially successful people have given to society versus a convicted murderer on death row (some who have already been vaccinated). However, fairness is not a sound criteria to follow either for vaccine distribution. If citizens are all equal, the most fair thing to do would be to have a lottery for distribution of the vaccine. But medically this would fail miserably, as it would arbitrarily help some who don't need help, while passing on others who are in dire need. The result would be more deaths and contagion than ever.

But there is a solution that is both fair and functional: Along with freely giving out the vaccine doses to the public, I think there should simultaneously be a small government sponsored private market for the vaccine—maybe just 5% percent of the total available doses. And all proceeds of this private market would go to increasing the speed of the distribution of the remainder of the vaccines to the public.

Think about it: Many well-to-do people might pay $5000 or even $10,000 for a dose. If even just one million people opted to pay for it, an extra $10 billion dollars would be created to help fight coronavirus. And people like myself would get vaccinated immediately, instead of waiting four more months, or maybe even until mid-summer.

One reason to create a small private vaccine market is also to respect game theory. If there's a new, much deadlier variant of the virus, or a terrible natural disaster strikes America, it will be the wealthy that our government again relies on to pay for the majority of its services (70 percent of income taxes are paid by the top 10% of American earners). Therefore, it's paramount we offer the biggest taxpayers a solution to get them vaccinated quickly so they will be financially viable for the country if needed. It's the same reason why during airplane emergencies, adults are told to put on their oxygen masks first, and then only afterward instructed to help those around them. In times of crisis, people and society function best when the most capable are operating at their strongest, so they have the endurance and will to help others.

Most of America will disagree with my arguments in this opinion essay. They will shout from the rooftops that high taxpayers don't deserve special privileges. But what if in this instance, the special privilege of a small private vaccine market helped fight the coronavirus while also strengthening America for its next emergency? I believe those that offer the most financially in America must be protected so that they can continue to serve society as a whole and carry the country forward.

****

CHAPTER IV: THE *PSYCHOLOGY TODAY* INTERVIEWS CONDUCTED BY ZOLTAN ISTVAN (2013-2017)

25) Wanted: A New Psychology; Interview with Futurist Gray Scott

Our civilization is being rapidly transformed through advancing science and technology. Despite this transformation, I feel most people are lagging behind philosophically, culturally, and psychologically when it comes to understanding and believing what is possible for human beings. Last week, I sent Gray Scott some questions so we could continue our dialogue. Here are my questions and his answers:

Q. Gray, we once discussed how a new psychology could be beneficial for society in regards to its understanding of the future and advancing technology. Can you elaborate your thoughts on this and why this might be desired?

A. We are experiencing unbelievable technological and psychological exponential change on this planet. We need a new set of psychological skills to cope with this change. Our world looks very different culturally, psychologically, and environmentally than it did 15 years ago. The mobile revolution has dramatically changed our world view, empowered women, and increased our empathy. Corrupt governments have been toppled and wars avoided because our species has become so digitally connected.

Negative and pessimistic views of technology have always existed. I can just imagine some pessimistic Sumerian in 3500 B.C. screaming about the evils of the wheel. We still deal with this fear based psychology in modern culture. Technology will mirror the culture and the psychology creating it. We need new psychological scaffolding to work with. Less fear and more optimism. A more holistic overview of how we look at ourselves and these new technological advancements could transform our planet.

I would love to see a future filled with abundance for everyone, however, we will not achieve this utopia until our cultural shadow-self is integrated. Taking psychological ownership of our fear is the first step. Technology is just a reflection of the deep unconscious cultural mind.

Q. What are some of the hang-ups you see with the current psychology that society seems to be stuck in when it comes to topics like transhumanism and radical life extension ideas?

A. Some people are hung up by fear. They are frightened of the changes they see around them. They are operating on old religious beliefs, old mythologies, and old information. The new techno-generation or transhuman generation are not buying it. They want to thrive. They want to live hundreds of years. They are not waiting on a rapture, doomsday, or cancer. They want utopia and they want it now. How can any culture be psychologically sound if we are told that we are "only human?" We have been conditioned to be frightened of our power, our love, our worth. Watch a child play and you will see real power. They are fearless. We are taught to desire the death wish, and it is not natural. Immortality may be impossible, but imagine what humanity could learn if we all lived 700 years. We could travel deep into utopia and beyond. We are experiencing a shedding of old psychological, political, and religious references. We could call it a psyco-digital-moulting.

Q. What are some good methods for getting society to embrace a new psychology for dealing better with the future?

A. One method is to seek out social support systems that are open and techno-positive. We need psychologists, elected representatives, and teachers to fully embrace technology. Transhumanism gives us a chance to unleash our biological and digital imagination into the material world. We can use bio-hacking and brain computer interface devices to allow people to walk again, see again, or communicate again. Showing the positive impacts of technology will help society embrace a new set of skills. The future is inclusive, not exclusive.

Q. I feel like technology is expanding very quickly, but human culture and psychology are not keeping up with it. How long can this go on before this discrepancy seriously hurts our species?

A. The technological singularity has been predicted to happen around 2045 so I would say that is our make or break time. As a futurist-philosopher, I am fascinated by the future of psychology. We have already crossed the threshold into the unknown. If we do not educate ourselves psychologically, we will face huge catastrophes in the near future. Digital outliers, like the elderly, Luddites, and poverty stricken will have a harder time understanding the new techno-psychology. Imagine a world filled with clones or artificially intelligent robots that can pass the "Turring Test" of believability. Are psychologists talking about the near future issues of robotic romance, digital-death remorse, or clone envy? Sounds like science fiction, but it is closer than most people would believe.

Q. How can the media play a better role in bringing forth a new psychology of the future and advancing technology?

A. Media consumption is no longer a passive experience. We touch, pinch, and swipe our way through the media world today. This interactive experience of seeking out knowledge and getting media from our social networks allows an entirely new psychology to emerge.

The way we consume media has radically shifted in the last 15 years. We can "binge-watch" entire seasons of shows in one day now that we have YouTube and Netflix. We can create individual "programming" based on our own psychological needs and desires.

The major media networks need to focus more on the positive implications of technology and less on dystopian fears. The people in the media need to be information leaders. They need to educate and enlighten. Our cultural amygdala is worn out. No more terror alerts. No more fear. We are ready for a higher road.

****

26) Transhumanist Nikola Danaylov Faces Tragedy with Resolve

Nikola Danaylov, founder of *Singularity Weblog* and a popular voice of the transhuman movement, recently had his world shaken when three close family members died within a period of three weeks.

Here's the start of a blog he wrote last month detailing his tragedy:

"In the past three weeks I had three deaths in the family: First, my aunt died suddenly from pancreatic cancer. Then my dad had a burst brain clot. And a few hours ago my grandmother had a stroke. All in all, I haven't had so much death since my mother passed away when I was 14-years-old..."

Yesterday, I had the chance to interview Nikola. I want to share his transhumanist views on death:

Q. Nikola, it sounds like you've been through a nightmare. We all fear such a thing with our loved ones. Three close members of your family died within a few weeks of each other. What are your thoughts and feelings about these deaths?

A. In all three cases, death was sudden and unexpected. Each one of those would be a hard and painful thing to go through, even on its own. Enduring all three within such a short period of time had brought immense sadness and a helpless feeling of eternal loss and tragedy. I had no time say good bye or get ready in any way. I was just shocked by the events.

Q. You have been an admired member of the transhuman and life extension communities for many years. You've interviewed everyone from Noam Chomsky to Natasha Vita-More to Jacque Fresco. Your website, blog, and podcasts are very popular. Can you tell us if these family deaths you've just experienced have shaken your views on transhumanism and mortality? Or perhaps they have reinforced them?

A. If anything those recent deaths have reinforced my convictions because they brought home the fact that Transhumanism is no mere theory. It is the only rational recourse that we have to fight death and make a real difference for people—and to try to alleviate suffering for everyone.

People have sought a way to defeat death since Gilgamesh. And for many millennia this void has been filled with religion—which promises life after death. But the only rational path to defeating death is science. It's the only path that has demonstrated that we have made measurable progress towards extending healthy life-spans—and that we can eventually defeat death.

Q. What are some of the greatest scientific and technological challenges facing the human race when it comes to people overcoming their mortality?

A. In some sense death is a technical problem—a hardware malfunction. And I have no doubt that eventually humanity will find a number of technical solutions. Whether it happens in a few decades or centuries is really not so important in the grand scheme of things. The timing is more of a selfish issue related to particular individuals such as you and me. But what is more important than whether the two of us will personally survive death or not, is the outcome for humanity in general.

As a philosopher I rarely see the greatest challenges as merely technological and/or scientific. Yes, science and technology are very, very important, but in the end, it is their application that makes all the difference for good or for bad, for life or for death. And so I believe that we ought to engage the ethics of defeating death even before we have the technical means to do so; it is important that we challenge and eventually change the age-old acceptance of death as inevitable. For example, we used to take for granted that when someone got a heart-attack they will inevitably die very soon thereafter. Then we figured out how to do by-pass surgeries (or whole heart transplants), and now people can have high-standards of living for decades after something that used to condemn them to death. Thus, the inevitability that one dies during or shortly after a heart attack is gone. And there are countless other examples like that. So what we need to do is create the ethical momentum and moral framework which will provide impetus for an explicit, vocal, global, coordinated, and focused scientific quest against death. Especially death from old age. That is the first step on the path towards overcoming our mortality. The rest will come in time through scientific persistence and focused effort.

Q. You have written that "One day humanity will write Death's obituary." The majority of the world's population does not see that as a good thing—mostly because it counters their religious beliefs where death is an integral part of their faith. Can you tell us what needs to be done so that one day everyone will welcome writing death's obituary?

A. Most religions see death as inevitable. Yet, they also promise another life after death. And people rarely question the ethics of eternal life after death, as envisioned by major religions.

It is generally assumed it is a good thing to be resurrected like Jesus allegedly was. So if we do not object to everlasting life as promised by religion, why object to extended healthy life-spans as promised by science? After all, it is science that has made a measurable difference in both improving the quality of our life and its duration, not religion.

We humans are material beings made of atoms. We are sophisticated biological machines made of many complex parts. But in time, and with the help of science, we are learning more and more about how those machines work and how we can fix them. Today, nobody thinks twice about getting a cardiac bypass, or a pacemaker, or a Cochlear implant. Eventually most (and probably all) medical conditions will succumb to the ever growing body of scientific knowledge that we are accumulating. This is the nature of scientific progress. Sooner or later it will happen. So the more important question is: "How do we make life the default option?"

Since time immemorial, death has been the default position of which life is just the deviation. But so have been ignorance and darkness. And just like a single candle can dispel 10,000 years of darkness, knowledge can illuminate and dispel our age-old presumptions about death and its inevitability. So why not turn the equation upside down? Why should death be different than flying, instant communication, or going to Mars and beyond? Why shouldn't death die?

At the very least, death from old age could (and would) be defeated. And so death would become an accident, a tragic deviation of the norm. Not the other way around, as it is now.

There is a difference between walking the way and knowing the way. It is one thing to become immortal beings, it is another to be good at it. As we stumble into the future we are eventually going to resolve all the technical issues related to death. The ethical ones may turn out to be harder and longer lasting. So I think that scientists, philosophers, and laymen alike will need to start thinking about the ethics of defeating death as if we've already done it.

Q. What are your final thoughts in this interview?

A. It is said that: "Those who cling to life die, and those who defy death live." So let us not merely cling to life but be bold and defy death outright. Let us embrace our mortal challenge and be loud and clear about it. Let us declare that we want to bring "Death to Death!" and live our lives with the explicit knowledge that by doing so, even if we personally lose that battle, collectively we will eventually win the war. One day, humanity will write Death's obituary.

****

27) Gennady Stolyarov: A Children's Book Ponders Death

As a transhumanist, I was pleased to discover the nonfiction children's book Gennady Stolyarov II and his wife Wendy Stolyarov recently created and published. It's called *Death is Wrong*. Mr. Stolyarov is the author, and Mrs. Stolyarov is the illustrator.

B. J. Murphy, an advisor for the Lifeboat Foundation and a well-known writer for the respected think-tank Institute for Ethics and Emerging Technologies (IEET), recently wrote a review of Death is Wrong. Speaking of conquering death in his review, Murphy writes:

I believe this wonderful children's book, provided by the Stolyarovs, is a very grand step forward in achieving this. Not too grammatically complex, and not too excruciatingly simplistic, Death is Wrong is a blunt dose of reality, quick to the punch and holding nothing back. This is the book I wish I'd have read as a young child.

I agree with Mr. Murphy's review. I thought the book was fun to read and important in what it tries to accomplish.

Yesterday, I contacted Mr. Stolyarov to do an interview with him about his new book. He has a long history with writing and artistic creation.

Q. Gennady, what made you want to write this children's nonfiction book? How long have you been thinking about it?

A. In a way, this project was incubating in my mind ever since I committed myself at the age of five to the struggle against senescence and death. Over the past several years, I have been deliberating about unique ways that I could improve the prospects of radical life extension in our lifetimes, despite not being a biologist or doctor. I realized that everyone learns about death as a child, yet there are virtually no resources explicitly enabling children to recognize that the first reaction of horror and sadness at the injustice of death is fully correct and should be a motivating force to remedy that injustice. This, combined with the fact that I happen to be married to the most talented illustrator I know, made the creation of this children's book a logical step to take.

Q. What is the main message of the book?

A. Death is wrong, and we should do all we can to fight it using reason, science, and technology. Life is wonderful, and there are amazing opportunities people can have only if they live much, much longer than they currently do. Moreover, the scientific facts suggest the feasibility of achieving major increases in longevity during our lifetimes, so that some of us might never die at all.

Q. Why should we worry about death? Why should we teach our kids that we can overcome it?

A. Death is the obliteration of one's very being – an entire universe snuffed out forever, with everything lost and not even a memory of one's experiences, thoughts, emotions, or achievements remaining. If life – each individual's life – is the greatest good, as is self-evident to me, then death, the opposite of life, is the greatest evil and should be fought with all our resources, since we lose everything if we lose life. It is especially important to communicate this message to children before they are inculcated with all of the excuses, rationalizations, and evasions about death which have been built up over millennia of human history in order to alleviate the understandable and justified anxiety that people have about their mortality. Because, unlike in earlier eras, radical life extension can become technically feasible in our lifetimes, we need as many children as possible to grow up being passionate about pursuing it, instead of excusing death or distracting themselves from its ever-looming threat.

Q. What ages do you feel the book is best for? Is it also for adults?

A. This book is great for most children ages 8 and older – but I am aiming to encompass as young an audience as I can. I am especially eager for ambitious, talented younger children to discover it. It would have been treasured by me when I was four, and even several precocious children who embrace the prospect of indefinite life extension can radically improve all of our chances. This book is certainly for adults as well, particularly those who have never stopped questioning the way things are and who continually try to improve the world in paradigm-changing ways.

Q. Where can readers find more about your book and more information about you?

A. *Death is Wrong* is available on Amazon in Kindle and paperback. The official homepage for *Death is Wrong*, where important developments will be posted, can be found on website *The Rational Argumentator*.

****

28) Interview with Transhumanism Advocate Riva-Melissa Tez

Women are rare in the transhumanism field. Riva-Melissa Tez is a shining light. For this reason, I was glad to meet Riva and ask her some questions on the future. Riva is one of the more visible and popular young female advocates of transhumanism and life extension. Originally, it was Riva's passion for philosophy that got her interested in the deeper implications of science and technology for the human race. Riva studied Philosophy at University College London and has a track record of entrepreneurship and social innovation. She is also the founder of Berlin Singularity, a group focusing on bringing and promoting pro-longevity and futurist discussions to mainland Europe. Now she is living in San Francisco and co-runs Kardashev Communications, a German/US consultancy group focusing on better communications and funding for emerging technologies.

Q. Riva, there aren't many women that are actively involved in the life extension and transhumanism fields. Can you tell me why that is? Do you think women want to use science and technology as much as men do to live indefinitely and upgrade their bodies?

A. There certainly aren't enough women in these fields. It seems to me to be more of a grass roots problem. Only in the last few years have I seen a real conscientious effort to encourage women into engineering and certain sciences. Now companies like Goldieblox are equipping little girls with pro-science toys to try and change that at an early age. I was lucky—my dad was an electrical engineering professor and would always allow me to come into his office and play with stuff. I don't think women are inherently disinterested; maybe it's that the sort of topics that inspire people into looking outside of the present and into future possibilities are mainly promoted to men by men.

Q. It's important for almost any movement to have approximately an equal amount of men and women working toward goals and developing strategy. How can we increase female participation in the transhumanist movement?

A. At our last Berlin Singularity event there were maybe 70 people—at least a third of which were females. The after-discussion had a completely different edge. Someone should start a group or movement to promote women into futurism. Hey, that's an idea! But I don't want to be stereotypical—people are people, regardless of gender—but I've noticed that when the crowd has more females than usual, the whole discussion takes a more humble and caring attitude, even with what the men say. We are such funny animals, I love it.

Q. Riva, you recently gave a great speech at the Apple store in Berlin. Can you tell us a bit about what you presented?

A. I was asked by Apple to give a speech about the topic of the Singularity. They chose the title "What is Singularity?" which I found a little off, a bit like approaching someone to give a presentation on "What is History?" But I described what different people mean by the term 'singularity.' And what I'm referring to is the potential power of technology—from Von Neumann to Vinge, Kurzweil to Teilhard De Chardin, although quite a lot of my talk was focused on Kevin Kelly's idea of a 'Technium.' I resonate a lot with what Kelly writes in 'What Technology Wants'—he has a more encompassing view that I appreciate for being considerably wider in perspective, regardless of whether you might think he is right or not. I studied philosophy so I'm drawn to the bigger questions, discussing humanity and technology in terms of what we might perceive their goals to be. As a result, I always end my talks encouraging people to read up on Nick Bostrom/Future of Humanity Institute or getting to know MIRI (Machine Intelligence Research Institute).

A proportion of my talk was spent introducing and explaining some progresses in NBIC (nano/bio/informative/cognitive) technologies. In particular, my talk centered on certain aspects of biotechnology and machine learning. But over the last year I've grown to question how completely unfathomable it is that more importance hasn't been placed on aging research. It took a little while for me to realize and debate my own biases around the topic of extending healthy lifespans. But by the end of it, once I was able to regard the aging process free from the shackles of my own biases, I found my previous thoughts absurd. So a considerable proportion of any talk I do now will cover how I came to change my mind, as well as an introduction to some of the research on tackling aging worldwide. People find longevity research so anti-humane and egocentric, so it's interesting to tackle those views. I wrote an article about that exact topic a few months ago for H+ Magazine.

Q. What are some of your personal and professional goals in the next five years?

A. There's not really a divide between my professional and personal life—I never 'clock off.' At first I wasn't sure how to apply myself, having been compelled by my philosophy degree and yet disappointed by it, so I ended up co-founding a children's company in my late teens and then a tech start-up in my early 20s. As I read more about emerging technologies, I found what I was looking for in terms of philosophy and the ability to have tangible tools for bettering the world. There's a real fire in me to drive innovation—I feel nostalgic about the future and want the world to catch up. So to ensure innovation gets pushed forward we need better communication and outreach for these fields. And in turn that drives support and funding. So in five years time I want to look back and see I've helped some technological dreams come to fruition in whatever way I can.

The only goal I've ever had personally is to buy a large old house and transform it into a wonderland for children. I very nearly got round to doing it with a friend a few years ago. I found a dilapidated 15th century castle in England and had all these ideas—to put a slide from the third floor to the ground floor, to build a chemistry lab, to have a petting zoo. Although just a side project, business wise it would provide busy city parents with a magical place to send their children on the weekends or during holidays, but really it would serve the purpose to allow me to foster children in care. I'm happiest surrounded by children. My first two companies were about kids. It's just a different type of futurism.

Q. What are the three most important goals that you believe the life extension and transhumanist movement should aim for in the next 25 years?

A. I'm going to say aims that everyone in the movement can contribute to—better outreach and a move towards a more intelligent approach to funding. But then, I'm going to go for something a bit more stark, which is a total upheaval of the current medical industry.

Firstly, the more people who know, understand and appreciate how powerful, exciting and opportunistic certain technologies are for humanity the better. But it's going to take more than organizing groups and promoting the discussion, not that I'm discrediting these. What I'm hoping for is certain scientific breakthroughs to act as catalysts, though we can all be individual catalysts also. As long as we can protect and help certain research, then if they get results, the discussion will automatically become more publicized. So the most important goal right now is to make sure ideas don't fall through. And the main issue I find there is ensuring enough funding goes to these tough and novel ideas. We need to work on changing how funding streams work because right now they're contradictory to innovation. That's not an easy thing at all, but at least in smaller realms right now people are targeting the issue. This is a focus of mine. And by its very nature, better funding and outreach will bring more talent and scope into the area.

I'd like to say that in 25 years, the current medical system will be completely revolutionized. I can't believe what people put up with right now, the whole industry runs on principles completely contradictory to our wellbeing. I'll do whatever it takes to play an active role in changing that. I reckon in 25 years we'll have more than just a firm grip on aging and aging related diseases, but have also completely changed public perspective on those issues and their importance. As well as that, I'm fascinated by neurotechnology and the discussions around consciousness. I look at psychology up until now and see the subjectivity of it all. The very essence of how we see humanity will change. And we're so lucky to be a part of it.

******

29) Interview with Transhumanist Activist Hank Pellissier

Transhumanism is an international movement that's rapidly growing. The word transhuman literally means beyond human. Transhumanists are known for promoting and using science and technology to further the possibilities of the human species. One of their main aims is to overcome biological death.

Recently, there's been an uptick in transhuman activism in America. Hank Pellissier, director of the Brighter Brains Institute, and the producer of the recent TRANSHUMAN VISIONS conference series has been helping to lead the charge. His opening conference event sold out at its February 1st venue in San Francisco; the second conference—TRANSHUMAN VISIONS 2.0 - East Bay—is scheduled for March 1 (Future Day) in Piedmont, which is near Oakland. I recently asked Hank a few questions about his intentions and ideals.

Q. Hank, I've heard you speaking about "transhuman activism." What exactly do you mean by that? What do you want to happen?

A. I live in San Francisco and I'm proud of the Bay Area for being a national leader in transhumanism, but we're far, far behind Russia and Israel. Moscow and Tel Aviv have had demonstrations and marches that promote radical life extension. Mobs of people gathering with signs in a city square or marching down avenues, handing out pamphlets. We need transhumanist student associations on college and high school campuses—organizing rallies, insisting on progress, disseminating ideas. Little meet-ups are fine, but larger gatherings would be more impactful. I would like to see transhumanist film festivals, immortality dances, and powerful "actions" like the ones that Femen and PETA do. We need transhumanist picnics in graveyards, transhumanist rock concerts in crematoriums, and wine tasting in transhumanist art galleries. An event on "Day of the Dead" would be interesting; we could call it "Day of the No-More Dead."

Q. What do you see as important transhumanist issues, besides radical life extension?

A. There are four issues that are important to me: health, education, brain enhancement, and cosmetic surgery.

Let's start by discussing health, for obvious reasons. The obesity rate in the USA is skyrocketing. I've read that it's headed towards 66% in some states by 2030. I think transhumanists should be leaders in nutrition, exercise, and general fitness. Natasha Vita-More and Max More, the keynote speakers in the March 1 event are excellent role models for this.

Next is education. We need stellar free schooling opportunities for every citizen in every age group. It's a government investment that pays off. We need universal preschool and highly-trained elementary and secondary teachers. We need enthusiasm for STEM subjects—right now, international students comprise only 5% of our college campus population but they get 55% of the science and engineering PhDs.

Last are brain enhancement and cosmetic surgery. Transhumanists need to quantify the benefits of "smart drugs" and promote them to the general public. My TRANSHUMAN VISIONS 2.0 conference will hand out free nootropics—150 packets containing a 3-day supply of CILTEP by NaturalStacks. Everyone wants to be intelligent so let's create smart drugs cost-efficiently and gobble them down for cognitive gain. I'm also in favor of government-funded cosmetic surgery. Everyone deserves to be beautiful, everyone deserves to be the gender they want, everyone deserves to have a face and body they're happy with.

All these items are worth fighting for, but to get them, we need to plan, scheme, organize, build trust, share contacts, and develop leadership skills. My conferences will eventually evolve into discussion-oriented symposiums where people can easily meet each other and network for causes.

Q. What inspired you to organize these conferences?

A. Transhumanists need face-to-face time to build friendships, develop projects, and plan strategy. We need community. Just friending, communicating, and bickering online in social media isn't enough. We need to eat, scheme, schmooze, flirt, argue and create the future together in a physical setting. I saw this happening at the first conference—people animatedly discussing philosophy, science, ethics, technology and entrepreneurial visions with each other. I want activism, momentum for transhumanism so that we can make political, technological, and economic gains together.

Q. That sounds good, but a conference every month? Is there really an audience for that?

A. Yes, there's definitely an audience for that. The first conference totally sold out. Many people were disappointed they couldn't get tickets. I know 37 of the ticket-holders traveled long distance to get to the event—from Seattle, Arizona, Texas,

Florida, New York, Russia, Israel, and England. Transhumanism is a vibrant social movement with accelerating enthusiasm for its ideas...a conference once a month with 100-200 people? That seems minimal. When we look at the powerful radical movements of American history—Revolutionary war, abolitionism, suffragettes, anti-Vietnam War, even the Occupy Movement—no one was saying, "Hey, let's just keep it to one conference a year." That would be silly.

Q. Do you have a final message for readers, Hank?

A. Sure! Transhumanism has an attractive agenda that strongly appeals to many people, so let's get it out there to the public, via public events! Let's proselytize, let's spread the techno-optimist message.

After March 1, Hank Pellissier has scheduled three additional conferences:

April 5 - EROS EVOLVING - the future of love, sex, marriage and beauty

May 10 - RELIGION AND TRANSHUMANISM

June 14 - WORLD RADICAL FUTURES

****

30) Exploring a New Type of Community: Zero State

Rapid advances in technology are paving the way for new ideas about the future, including those of the communities we live in. I had a chance to catch up with Amon Twyman, who is part of one such community that is exploring new directions for the betterment of humanity.

Q. Amon, What is Zero State?

A. Zero State (ZS) is a community that grew out of the transhumanist movement back in 2011. It's now part of a broad coalition of groups and movements that we call WAVE, referring to a coming wave of radical technological and social change. The basic ZS idea is to create networks of people and resources which could evolve into a distributed, virtual State. Right now there are only a few thousand ZSers (albeit well connected to much larger networks), but in a hypothetical full-blown Zero State there would be tens of millions or more, all supporting each other and being part of a single nation no matter where they live in the world. Our motto is "positive social change through technology."

Q. How does transhumanism relate to ZS?

A. Our core principles and ideas are deliberately compatible with transhumanism. That comes naturally, as ZS grew out of transhumanism and our most active "citizens" tend to self-identify as Transhumanists. That said, it's important to stress that people don't have to be transhumanists to join ZS. More generally, we consider ourselves to be a "Social Futurist" community, which is to say that we believe technological breakthroughs don't happen in a social vacuum. There are social, economic, and political issues which not only stubbornly continue to exist in the face of techno-optimism, but which are sometimes greatly exacerbated by technological change. In short, we believe that technology should be applied to improving the human condition on both physiological and societal levels.

Q. How can ZS help the world?

A. In the first instance, we are focused on helping ZS' citizens, or more accurately, helping them to help each other. An increasing number of people are finding themselves in need of help of one type or another these days, and we would like to demonstrate that mutual support is made more achievable than ever before thanks to the power of cutting-edge technologies. We tend to focus on bringing together people and ways to access current technologies such as meshnets, cryptocurrency, Virtual Reality and Artificial Intelligence, while exploring ideas such as longevity, super-intelligence & wellbeing, accelerating change, and direct democratic action to circumvent obsolete political institutions. Beyond working to help our own people, we actively work to support the wider network of like-minded groups and believe that compassionately, intelligently applied technology has the potential to improve the lives of everybody in the world.

Q. How did you come to be the founder of ZS?

A. My background is in a combination of psychological research (consciousness and decision making, Artificial Intelligence) and digital & performing arts. Although I'd read my fair share of science fiction as a kid, I decided I was a transhumanist while studying at university, after reading "Mind Children" by Hans Moravec. Over time, my various interests in art, science, transhumanism, and contemporary social/political issues coalesced into a coherent worldview, and I eventually decided to form an organization to pursue these ideas. The result, Zero State, was heavily informed by my experience as a co-founder of the UK Transhumanist Association, which has since evolved into Humanity+ UK. I started building WAVE, the broader network ZS is part of, two years later. That was once we'd had time to realize that there was a bigger picture emerging; a large number of like-minded groups forming to address a vast array of specific issues with a common outlook. That common outlook is characterized by technological savvy, distaste for old thinking and limits, and a keen awareness of social issues.

A. What does the future hold for ZS?

Q. ZS-affiliated project groups continue to work on developing tools for our members. A lot of these projects are collaborative and many have a distinctly transhumanist flavor, such as experimentation with Transcranial Direct Current Stimulation (using electrical charge to help concentration—work being done in collaboration with Dirk Bruere and Andrew Vladimirov). Some of the projects seem more like simple fun than serious experimentation at first glance—such as the ZSers building Minecraft environments in which to test their AI software—but that's half the point; For people to do something useful and have fun at the same time. Our most vigorous efforts are currently going into WAVE, expanding the wider, networked context in which ZS operates, doing what we can to help out like-minded groups. We've been establishing connections with large networks, such as The Zeitgeist Movement and an emerging coalition of online transhumanist organizations. We live in extremely exciting times, with lots of rapid change both good and bad, and it looks like Zero State will soon get its chance to help people help each other in that brave new world. If you believe in the promise of technology, the importance of social justice, and the power of community building then feel free to jump in and join the fun!

****

31) Women in STEM, Transhumanism, and a New Author to Watch

Given that today is Mother's Day, I wanted to use my blog to interview Nicole Sallak Anderson, a computer scientist, mother, and novelist. Her new science fiction novel *eHuman Dawn* is well-written, exciting, and full of transhumanist themes. I recently had the pleasure of meeting Nicole when she spoke at a Transhuman Visions conference in Piedmont, California.

Q. Nicole, what led you to pursue a career in computer science?

A. When I was 12, Apple computer donated several Mac II computers to my school, as well as money to pay for a computer science teacher. Because I was on the Math Counts team, I was pulled out of math class with a few other kids and taught to program. I loved it. The first programs I wrote were short, animated stories for the Kindergarten children. Oh the graphics in those days!

As I began to apply for colleges, my heart's desire was to go into journalism and creative writing, but my father refused to pay for it, stating college was an investment on his part, one that should guarantee a living wage so that he didn't have to take care of me. So I thought about my other hobby…writing software. That's when I chose to pursue a degree in computer science and the rest is history.

Q. How did you become a novelist?

A. I never forgot my love of storytelling, and in my late twenties I began to write novels and short stories again. *eHuman Dawn* was the first to gain the attention of an agent. Three years ago, I had a dream in which I was living in a robotic body, and the government was powering down our cities in order to flush out terrorists. From there, the *eHuman Trilogy* was formed, beginning with eHuman Dawn.

Q. Was transhumanism always something you were interested in?

A. Technically, no. Until my dream, I didn't spend much time considering life-extension technologies. Yet, I've always believed in technology as an elegant servant in many ways. In addition, I've long felt that we've barely tapped into the power of the human mind and body. There's no reason we can't live to be 150 years old, we just haven't invested time and money into the problem of early death. On the contrary, our society invests heavily in the technologies of death and destruction, rather than in life and construction. Just look at our military budget vs. investments into high tech green energy, transportation or health systems. It's completely backwards.

Q. What does the transhumanism movement mean to you, and how does the *eHuman Trilogy* play a part?

A. To me, transhumanism means becoming more human and investing in humanity because we're important and we matter. Technologies that improve our memories, intelligence, and survival are of the utmost importance. Research into AI and how it can help manage our cities and our future civilization is crucial. Yet I also feel a sense of caution is important as well. If we invest in transhuman solutions because we fear death, we're incredibly vulnerable to manipulation by those who own the technologies. Many transhumanists claim that the human body is the most frail thing on earth, and that to live in a computer would be more secure. I disagree. That security will depend on who owns the energy source needed to power the computer our consciousness lives in. That someone could walk into a room and unplug me for any reason what-so-ever does not feel secure to me.

eHuman Dawn addresses these issues. I hope the novels will inspire an effort to make the movement towards immortality more robust and secure. Human rights issues must be addressed sooner than later.

Q. What is the main message in *eHuman Dawn*?

A. In a nutshell, I'd say the message is, "When you entrust your dreams, identity and immortality to technology, you entrust it to those who own that technology. Are those in charge of our society worthy of such power?"

Stopping research into transhuman and life extension technologies is NOT the answer. Nor is fearing those who wish to become immortal. This is going to happen at some point in our history, regardless of any resistance. I hope to bring a voice to the discussion surrounding consumer protections and rights.

For example, right now there's a huge debate on big data and what is done with it. What's private on the internet? What isn't?

Who owns the flow of information? Now is the time to set laws that protect the users from the producers, not later. What we decided to do in this post-Snowden era will guide us as we create networked houses, cities and, with time, humans.

Q. Why do you think so few women are interested in careers in technology and transhumanism?

A. When I was in grade school, the ratio of boys and girls interested in math and science seemed even. My small, Apple sponsored computer class in junior high was split 50-50. But when I got to college, I was one of five women who graduated in computer science that year. Often I was the lone female, surrounded by men. Which to me, wasn't a bad thing. I love men. I love their logic and sturdy emotions.

My female friends weren't interested in my work. Nor the books I read. I'm really not sure why, but one instance stands out in my mind. I went to an all girls high school, and being smart and intelligent was encouraged. During my senior year, the school became co-ed and for the first time, all the honors math and science classes were mixed. I remember the first week, when the teacher asked us a question, the only hands that went up were the boys. Girls I'd known to be incredibly outgoing in class were now silent, looking down instead of at the teacher.

It shocked me and to this day, I don't understand it. Perhaps somewhere women get the message that to be smart is to be unattractive. Combine that with the sentiment that only geeks like math and science (another destructive stereotype) and you find the higher you go in such subjects, the less women participate.

As for me, my intellect and ability to reason have always been very important. I couldn't imagine my life without science fiction, algebra and computers. Picking up a book on quantum physics or reading about the Bitcoin revolution are exciting to me, even if I am, "a girl."

Transhumanism falls into this category of the geek. The good news is, I think more and more millennial females are okay with being seen as a nerd. As that happens, perhaps even more men will let go of the stereotype as well, allowing a whole new generation of people to participate in bringing humanity forward with new, exciting, technological advancements.

******

32) TransEvolution, Transhumanism, and Daniel Estulin

I recently had the opportunity to interview Lithuanian-born Daniel Estulin, an award winning investigative journalist and author of international bestseller *The True Story of the Bilderberg Group*, which has sold over seven million copies worldwide and has been translated into 42 languages. Daniel has also recently written *TransEvolution – The Coming Age of Human Deconstruction*, which, among other things, explores how the elite of the world plan to use transhumanism to maintain their power and status. *TransEvolution* is well-written and well-researched, and an intriguing perspective of the future. I recommend it. While I don't agree with some of the ideas in the book, I was glad to read it and explore the perspectives presented by Mr. Estulin, who ultimately is a man full of challenging and bold ideas.

Q. Daniel, thank you for doing this interview. Let's begin with this question: Why did you write *TransEvolution*?

A. Back in 2005, I came across a very important draft which was discussed at the Bilderberg conference in Rottach-Egern, Germany. It is called Strategic Trends Report 2007-2036, a secret source document on the future of humanity. This 91-page report is a blueprint for the United Kingdom´s future strategic national requirements through the analysis of key risks and future shocks to the world's financial, economic, political, demographic, and technological areas and markets. Once I read what my Bilderberg sources gave me, I realized that I was looking at the elite's plans for the future of humanity.

Q. Your famous book on the Bilderberg Group portrays the elite as intentionally attempting to dictate policy and the future of the world. Do you think the elite are planning on using transhumanist technology to do so?

A. We are living at the cusp of the greatest evolutionary change in the history of mankind. The generation of our children, many who are teenagers today, is the last, truly human generation of human beings on planet Earth. Our grandchildren will be transhuman children, post-human children, man-machines, cyborgs—beings who are not totally human as a result of synthetic biology.

With Bilderberg it was easy. You knew that someone faceless was doing something in the financial markets, coup d'etat, etc, so once I exposed these people, we suddenly knew their names and their deeds. But, with this, all is different. The elite forever controlled knowledge, but with the information revolution today, an Indian sitting in a tree in the middle of a rainforest in Bolivia with a laptop, an internet connection, and Google, has access to everything the secret societies had hidden from us since the beginning of time.

So, the elite have figured out that the best way to break this divide between them and us is through technology. On the one hand, they are destroying the world's economy on purpose, sending us all to Hell in a hand basket. Why? Because progress and development is directly proportional to population density. So, if there is technological progress for all of us, there are going to be more people on Earth. More people means less resources, which means for the elite to survive, we have to die. This is what's behind deindustrialization, zero growth, and demand destruction mentality. Look at Detroit. This is an example of what is being done on purpose. Except the elite want Detroit to be the poster child for the world's deindustrialization.

On the other hand, they are using trillions of their dollars to develop far reaching advanced technology that literally will control the world.

Q. Is there a way to make technology of the future accessible to all people, regardless of wealth or status?

A. Obviously. We can't survive without technology and technological innovation in the age of greater and greater population density around the world. However, technology is a double edged sword. For example, thanks to modern technology, you can have a world famous brain surgeon in Philadelphia operating on a little girl with brain cancer in Indonesia without leaving his office. And on the other hand, you can have a four-star US general at the Pentagon operating a drone that will kill someone or many someones half-way around the world, also without leaving his office.

Let me give you another example. Space exploration. The Moon harbors enormous resources that we can use on Earth, including titanium, aluminum, and iron. Water from asteroids can fuel an in-space economy. The Moon has a decisive advantage relative to the Earth, in the purification of those metals, which are always found in raw minerals that contain a lot of oxygen. On Earth, the molten metal must be placed in a vacuum to achieve oxygen extraction, thereby obtaining the best mechanical and anti-corrosive qualities possible. But to create that vacuum is very costly.

Because the Moon has no atmosphere, the vacuum is free, and of a much better quality than anything we have been able to create on Earth. With a perfectly purified lunar titanium, we could build bridges on Earth that would last forever. All this is possible only if the metal purification is achieved on the Moon.

Furthermore, the Moon harbors important reserves of Helium-3, very rare on Earth, which is the ideal element to realize nuclear fusion ... The very same source of energy which is abundant in much of our Solar System and on the Moon. In fact, there is enough fuel on the Moon to meet the present energy needs of the entire Earth for close to 2,000 years. Helium-3 is a natural decay product of radioactive tritium and is the most effective, most efficient thing for the production of thermonuclear weapons.

So, we can use the abundance of Helium to provide energy to the entire planet or use the resources on the Moon to kill us all.

Q. What is the worst case scenario with technology in the future? Could we lose our humanity? Does this bother you?

A. The rise of the machines is here. We are facing the time when an unconscious evolution period is almost finished. And we come to the new period when a controlled human evolution can and will happen. Technological progress will be concentrated on making a new body for the human being. The plan is to incrementally move the human mind into more disembodied and futuristic vehicles: first a humanoid robot controlled entirely by a human brain via brain-machine interface, then a conscious human brain transplanted into a humanoid robot, then consciousness uploaded to a computer, and finally a hologram that contains a full conscious human mind.

We are witnessing an unparalleled explosion in scientific knowledge. Because of the synergy, the interplay of three great revolutions: quantum, computer, and biotech revolution, we have learned more in the past 50 years than in all of human history. We have many marvels of science, like the Internet, telecommunication satellites, laser beams, radio, television, microwaves, biotechnology—even a structure of a DNA molecule. All of it, ultimately, comes from quantum theory.

We have the means through genetics, robotics, information technology, and nano technology to control matter, energy, and life itself. We have never seen anything like this before, and it is raising profound questions about what it means to be human. The intense cross pollination between the computer, biotech, and quantum revolutions will give us unprecedented power in the 21st Century.

Q. What are working on now? What can we expect in the future from Daniel Estulin?

A. Because of the large success of *TransEvolution – The Coming Age of Human Deconstruction*, I will start working on the follow up that will take the reader beyond the 2045 period into the second half of the 21st Century. All of it will be based on hard evidence and private documents that I got my hands on from government sources.

****

33) Interview with Transhumanist Biohacker Rich Lee

Transhumanism—the rapidly growing international movement that aims to use radical science and technology to significantly improve the human being—has many fascinating fields of study. One of my favorite areas is biohacking. I recently had a chance to chat with Rich Lee, a leading biohacker whose upgrades and experiments to his body are both impressive and courageous. His exploits have been featured in *CNN, The Guardian, Popular Science, The Huffingon Post*, and many other well-known media sites.

Q. Rich, thanks for doing this extensive interview. Let's start with the basics: What is biohacking?

A. Biohacking has a lot of different definitions depending on who you ask, and I haven't seen a definition that I like 100%, and that includes my own. Defining what actions constitute a "biohack" is even harder in recent years because the terms hack and hacker get substituted to describe a million different activities just like the terms "Smurf" and "Smurfy" are used by people in the Smurf Village culture. Viewing these different definitions pulled from dictionaries, wikis, and community websites gives hints about biohacking history and speaks volumes about the current state of biohacking, and the transitioning attitudes people have toward it. Here are some current definitions:

1) Biohacking is the intentional manipulation of a living system to accomplish a desired result.

2) Biohacking is the practice of engaging biology with the hacker ethic

3) To use systems thinking, science, biology, and self-experimentation to take control of and upgrade your body, your mind, and your life.

4) The creation of genetically-engineered organisms in makeshift gene laboratories.

5) A biohacker is anyone who dabbles in the field of GMOs and genetic-cloning without proper authority or a real humanistic vision.

6) The activity of exploiting genetic material experimentally without regard to accepted ethical standards, or for criminal purposes.

The first three definitions come from within the biohacking community, and the last three are civilian definitions. The view from within is very different from without, and I noticed something weird and revealing about the first three definitions versus the second three. The very topmost definition was mine, but a few days after becoming irritated by a guy at a party who introduced himself as a "biohacker" when I think he should have said "vitamin cult disciple", I realized that technically a case could be made to include his brand-specific regimen of self-righteous supplement ingestion, using my own definition. Other definitions from within biohacking also seemed vague, and some of those definitions have even been refined in the last few years, but now I notice that the newer versions (which I prefer) somehow became even less defined than previous versions! This bothered me because in my mind I thought that my idea of what biohacking was and wasn't had become much clearer than it was five years ago, and instead of becoming more concrete, my personal definition was so nebulous that it could be interpreted to include anyone who brushes their teeth. So if your daily routine involves covering thousands of fine nylon rods in certain enzymes that you use to hack bacteria populations inside your oral cavity, then congratulations! You are one of us by my definition. Broader acceptance in the community might require you to use open source toothpaste.

My definition was constantly evolving to accommodate all of the new possibilities I was encountering in the community and in science. So my original definition went something like "enhancing or augmenting the human form with technology to overcome the genetic limitations imposed by the flesh." I extended my definition of biohacking beyond my own body after seeing a mycologist who used fungus to create large lightweight bricks in a matter of days. My initial goals involved replacing biological components with bionic ones, but it turns out that in many cases biology offers a lot of advantages over mechanical or electrical options, so I modified the word "technology" in my definition to incorporate organic solutions. Personal genetic modification became a consideration, but genetic engineering can also be done on the bacteria that populate our microbiome, or to produce chemicals and drugs outside the body. You get the point.

Compare this to the definitions others have created. Those three definitions are based on ignorance. They get real specific about which tools a biohacker uses or what motivates them. Bioterrorism and biohacking are indistinguishable by some definitions and might include or exclude malevolent botanists and neurologists from their definition. But this is the view from outside of biohacking, and it gets used in the news, government memos, and biotech press releases.

These sentiments are changing thanks in large part to the DIY Bio movement. Communal biohacking spaces are opening in cities all over the globe, bringing together citizen scientists of all experience levels to work on projects, teach techniques, and share a passion for biology. It is a great place to learn. One day you might find yourself replicating proteins, using algae to produce your own biofuel at home, identifying the fungus that is ruining your garden, or learning how easy it is to hack common yogurt to produce a lifetime supply of some prescription drugs like Prozac. Someday the historians of the future will look back to measure the social impact of certain movements and we will honor the people who nurtured the DIY Bio movement in these early days. Thanks in large part to them, biology is no longer a mystic craft practiced exclusively by biotech scientists and academics in designated labs. Knowing about biology and owning a home lab does not make you a bioterrorist. Having a strong global biohacking community and knowledgeable population that knows how to do things for themselves also helps to hedge against the wild social upheavals that may occur when one class of citizen is denied access to vital medicines or treatments of extreme evolutionary importance. The DIY threat is going to become a major factor in keeping the price of future goods low.

The Quantified Self movement is huge too. These guys helped me refine the way I was doing things and really drove home the importance of being able to measure the things you want to change. QS has a huge amount of interesting stuff for the self-experimenting biohacker types. The Quantified Self community also encourages real life meet ups and there is probably already a group in your area you can go check out.

The subculture of biohackers I belong to have been given the nickname "Grinders." The term was actually borrowed from modern video game culture. "Grinding" referred to the methodical act of improving one's character within a game, trying to maximize a skill or stat. In Grinder culture we have a similar attitude toward self improvement, but we often blend this with very individualistic things like extreme body modification. We tend to work with existing tech, and none of us are holding out for the AI messiah or nanobots. We make and install our own implants.

Q. How did you get into it?

A. I grew up in a very religious family and was taught from an early age that my life was going to be short because the Lord was coming to melt everyone and take me to heaven. This had a huge impact on the way I viewed the future and my own potential. I couldn't imagine being alive to see my next birthday, or going to college, or starting a family. I was 100% on board with the idea of dying as soon as possible. Imagining a future where that didn't happen was almost impossible. This same derangement skewed what I thought humanity could accomplish too. An effort to fund a manned flight to Mars within twenty years might have amused me, but I would never consider donating to something like that because the time to completion was too far out. All long term planning seemed like a waste of time, and short term goals were hard to commit to because next week's apocalypse has a way of overshadowing everything else on your calendar. I'm still paying the price for short sighted life choices I made as a teen. Anyway, the end didn't come. Later I would discover that religious leaders had been unsuccessfully predicting the end of days throughout history and I wondered how many other kids now and throughout time dreamed of the rapture instead of rockets. I run into these kids all the time and most aren't as extreme as I was, and there is definitely a spectrum, but no part of this spectrum is healthy. It makes me mad to think about the greater impact that this type of thinking has had on humanity.

I became an atheist in my mid-twenties and had to reconcile the fact that nobody was coming to save me. Eventually I replaced religion with futurism. I felt that science and technology offered a tangible alternative to all the things religion had promised me. Fantasies of heavenly immortality were replaced with hopes of life extension drugs, angelic wings were replaced with jetpacks and flying cars. I took comfort reading articles about the exponential advancement of technology and various breakthroughs in modern medicine.

My grandmother passed away in 2008. She left behind a tub of magazines that spanned the 1950's through the eighties. I instinctively flipped to the science and technology sections of these magazines and was confronted with headlines about how modern medicine would cause humans to have 200 year lifespans by the year 2000, or that a family vacation to the moon would be common in the year 1995. Later I'd discover that futurists had been predicting these things for ages. Then I wondered how many people from previous eras had died waiting for that flying car, or expected to live to be 200. For me there was no difference between the blind faith I put in science and the one I had put in religion. I also noted that just because something has been discovered it doesn't guarantee that it will be available. The jetpack has been around since the 1960's, so why don't you have one? I was gripped with a new kind of panic, and I decided I would have to get involved to make it happen. This led me to biohacking, and eventually to transhumanism.

Although I was philosophically aligned with transhumanists, I found most of my interactions with them infuriating because there seemed to be too much cheerleading and not enough working. When I talked about implants I had, some transhumanists would squirm and ask "why don't you just wait for the singularity or nanobot or brain uploading?" Attitudes toward Grinders and self-experimenting biohackers have changed a lot since then though, but I still encounter these passive sentiments a lot. I just focus on tangible tech, and I don't treat it like a hobby. I think of it as an arms race.

As far as projects go, biohackers might have certain interests and priorities that they favor over others. So the neuro/cog guys might make their own tDCS or TMS brain stimulation devices, EEGs, try different nootropic substances, things like that. Self enhancing biohackers can typically be split into two groups: maximizers & beyonders. I made up these terms. An athletic type maximizer works to maximize his/her existing hardware and might pursue TENS assisted strength training, steroids, etc. A Beyonder might make an exoskeleton or something like that, abandoning their hardware limitations in favor of a tool that lets them lift stuff well above normal human limits. Microbiome guys might study ways to alter bacteria inside their body to do something cool. One guy wanted to hack odorous microbes found in his sweat glands to smell like watermelon instead of body odor. I'd try it. There are guys into cybernetics, optogenetics, and gene therapies. Anyway, there are lots of areas of focus and they can usually be attacked from different angles and on multiple levels of the stack. I tend to have three main areas of focus: Sensory expansion, need removal, and novel functionality.

Q. What is an example of novel functionality?

A. I think it would be cool to have LED implants under my skin that could be turned on or off. My friend Tim had an implant with LEDs and it was a cool effect. I have lots of other ideas too. One of them is a device that vibrates and gets implanted where you might expect it to and will probably improve sex.

Q. How about need removal? Please explain.

A. Maslow's hierarchy of needs has been a personal hit-list of things I'd like to change for myself and humanity. To me it represents the worst aspects of being human. I'd guess that the majority of horrific acts of violence committed by humans can be traced back to some need on that chart. How pathetic is it that we crave the acceptance of other humans? That our sanity breaks down in conditions of solitary confinement? Can we imagine removing some of these needs and still feel human? What would it be like if you never had to sleep? If humans could supply themselves with fresh clean water by extracting it from the air they breathe? What if we could use biology that utilizes nitrogen in the air instead of the soil to supply all of our essential amino acid needs? It would put a major dent in hunger. What if we could use technology to destroy Maslow's Hierarchy of needs tier by tier? Would we develop new needs? What would those be? These are questions that keep me up at night and drive many of my biohacking ambitions.

Q. Explain sensory expansion.

A. This is big in the Grinder community. Most people start off by implanting magnets in their fingertips, which gives you the ability to feel magnetic fields. Your fingertips have lots of nerve endings jammed into one area and they are really sensitive to stimuli. Magnets twitch or move in the presence of magnetic fields, and when you implant one in your finger you can really start to feel different magnetic fields around you. So it is like a sixth sense. At first you will be waving your hand around appliances, probing fields like someone looking for a light switch in the dark. After a few days or weeks you will almost forget you have the implant because your brain has fully incorporated the sense into your normal world experience. When you sleep you will notice that even your dreams have changed to include the sense. You can now perceive an otherwise invisible world.

This makes many curious about all of the other things happening around them that they can't see and they want more. So let's expand on the magnet thing. We can buy all kinds of different sensors to detect heat, radiation, radio signals, wifi, whatever you want. If we wrap a wire around our implanted finger and attach that wire to our new sensor, we find that the wire creates a small magnetic field to the beat of the sensor. This of course makes our magnet twitch, and now we can feel heat from a distance, feel wifi, or whatever.

Why limit ourselves to feeling these sensations? We have other senses we can induce synesthesia in. I got some media attention in June of 2013 after I implanted headphones in my tragus to do just that. I had some practical reasons for doing this in addition to my thirst for exploration. A few years earlier I suddenly became legally blind in one eye. Lenses cannot correct it and my original eye doctor informed me that the other eye was likely to follow, at which point I would be legally blind, lose my job, etc. With this inevitability in mind I decided to be proactive. Ultrasonic rangefinders are devices used to determine how far away an object is. I knew that most blind people find acoustic variations help them identify the proximity of objects, so I figured I might be able to amplify this by converting rangefinder data into audio I could send wirelessly to my headphone implants. It turned out to be much more complicated than I thought, but that is a part of Grinding that I have come to appreciate. My setbacks lead me deeper into the rabbit hole of audiology where I discovered knowledge that has unlocked a thousand more possibilities.

I'd say that 25% of the people I talk to about sensory enhancement think it's really cool and some go get implants themselves. The other 75% will nod their head and hope the conversation ends or they laugh and ask "why would anyone want to feel magnetic fields?" I get asked that question so much, and I still find it hard to articulate. They usually point out that "you don't need it," to which I counter "what if you lost the ability to taste? You don't really need it to survive." Ask anyone with an implant how they would feel if they lost the implant, and almost all of them will tell you they would miss it. A small bit of richness would be missing from their life experience.

Visible light is but a tiny portion of the greater magnetic spectrum that we cannot see. If we modeled the entire spectrum as a road stretching from LA to New York, the amount of visible light that humans can see would equal a few nanometers. Humans, from our allegorical caves, have nonetheless managed to form and test theories about things at the edges of perception but these discoveries took thousands of years. Where would humans be now technologically if we never developed sight? How long would it take us to theorize the existence of the aurora borealis or to hypothesize about the existence of stars? This reduction of input obviously cripples the rate of input.

So is the opposite true? Would expanding our senses accelerate our advancement? My answer is yes. Some Grinder friends of mine formed a team called Science for the Masses to discover if they could biologically push human perception of visible light into the near-infrared spectrum. This is a small increase, around 6% above our current abilities. The impact is dramatic. The new light allows you to see through fog and haze, tinted windows, and some clothing. Stars can be seen during day hours. Subtle changes in blood flow can be seen under the skin, allowing anyone to detect circulation problems and find clots. Seeing blood flow takes some of the guesswork out of determining what mood your date is in and lying becomes nearly impossible. Imagine how this awareness would have altered human history, politics, art, courtship, and relationships. Does human psychology benefit in a world where sincerity and emotional context can be seen with the naked eye rather than hypothesized or conjured? The new layers of info I've detailed above are actually just the tip of the iceberg. The real magic of sensory expansion comes from finding deviations and surprises that don't fit within our scientific understanding because it makes us reconcile our mental models of the world with reality.

Some will find this thought experiment amusing. The biohacking team I mentioned earlier will be publishing their findings sometime this year and, depending on the results, humans could be seeing infrared within a few months, amusement will fade into reality, and mass adoption will lead to mass adaptation. The world might change because of four young punk biohackers who struggled and sacrificed to raise the mere $4,000 they needed to do this. If one biohacker project costing $4000 has the potential to alter the course of humanity, imagine the impact of the other 200 projects I didn't tell you about.

Sorry for the long winded response here. I always tell this story because it shows people a side of transhumanism that isn't talked about much. Ask most people what transhumanism is and they will bring up nanobots, life extension, AI, and mind uploading. Those things are swell, and I hope someday they get the billions of dollars they need for additional R&D so they can have a world changing product tested, approved, and ready to sell to rich people in the next 20 to 30 years so that people will start to take transhumanism seriously. But if there is one thing anyone remembers after reading this I hope it is this: There exists a small group of passionate grinders and biohackers who, despite having limited resources and few evangelists, tinker, test, and collaborate on a daily basis because they see transhumanism as a noble cause and a method to uplift mankind and that they have ambitious ideas for achieving this using affordable and existing technology they believe may change the world.

****

34) Author David Simpson Talks Transhumanism in Science Fiction

Q: David, your recent foreword to *The Robot Chronicles*, a short story collection featuring some of the biggest names in science fiction, seemed to herald the arrival of transhumanist/singularity science fiction as a dominant sub-genre. Full disclosure, I've written a well-known transhumanist novel myself, but for the sake of argument, couldn't we say that *Asimov's Foundation Series* was also transhumanist since it dealt with AI and robots? Mary Shelley's Frankenstein is an even older example of a novel about a scientist trying to achieve immortality. Given the history of these science fiction concepts, how can we say that transhumanism in science fiction is suddenly something new?

A: It's paradoxical for sure, and who doesn't love a great paradox? Issues like immortality, AI, robotics, and even more recently, virtual reality in the sub-genre of cyberpunk, have been around for decades (and centuries in the case of immortality and Frankenstein). But science fiction, perhaps more so than any other type of fiction, reflects the reality of the moment and the mood of the people. I'd argue there was a period beginning with the release of Star Wars in 1977 and ending with the attacks of September 11th, 2001, that was, looking back, a period of relative optimism, both in science fiction and in western culture as a whole. The *Star Wars* and *Star Trek* franchises, which both seemed to encourage dreaming positively about the future of humanity, were huge successes, not just on the big screen but also in television, comics, and fiction. I think science fiction was doing what it is best at, and that is inspiring people and influencing untold thousands of people to become scientists and dream of better futures. After 9/11, the mood of America and the world became, understandably, distinctly darker. This echoes what happened prior to Star Wars in 1977 as a result of the long and drawn out conflict in Vietnam. Similarly, the Iraq war certainly bred cynicism, and then just as it seemed we were ready to come out of the darkness, the global economy collapsed and the Great Recession commenced. As a result, popular science fiction has been mired in books and movies that reflect the times, so post-apocalyptic visions and dystopias became the rage. It's been a long, thirteen-year dark mood bordering on a depression that the world, only now in the late summer of 2014, seems to be threatening to emerge from. Serious setbacks in Russia and the Ukraine aside, the economy is rolling again, technology seems to be advancing with personal mobile computing revolutionizing our lives, and with companies like Space X talking about sending humans to Mars within fifteen years, it seems to be providing a ray of hope that perhaps we're about to get back to seriously moving the species forward in an exciting and optimistic way.

I think that's why my *Post-Human* series has had very close to 100,000 downloads on Amazon since the middle of March this year, because *Post-Human* is a transhumanist/singularity inspired adventure series that depicts a future of fantastic possibilities that people are just starting to realize is actually on the horizon and they're hungrily looking for stories about it. When Asimov was writing about similar themes, it was still just a little too far away to seem urgent, but the accelerating pace of information technology has changed all of that, and now transhumanist science fiction is posed to become the dominant sub-genre of science fiction, and in a way, what's old is new again.

Q. What would you say to someone who countered that a lot of things actually go wrong because of technology and science in the *Post-Human* series? Doesn't that make your series as negative as the post-apocalyptic books you're referring to?

A. A good friend of mine who used to be the Executive Director of the World Transhumanist Association (now Humanity+) and the founder of *H+ Magazine* is a big supporter of the *Post-Human* series and pointed out that, despite what he called the "necessary conflicts," the stories actually depict technology making people's lives better. I was so happy that he understood that drama is conflict. If I were to write a book about the fantastic technology that is on the horizon and nothing ever went wrong, then I'd really be writing a polemic, and polemics are rarely interesting. The truth is, strong AI, meaning AI that surpasses humans in intelligence, is going to be a game changer on a level not seen since humans evolved their neocortex, except that the first strong AI is likely to emerge in a matter of a few years rather than through thousands of years of evolution, and it's guaranteed to soar past human intellectual capability. It'll be an incredible moment, one that's been called our "last invention," and it's possible that the time period leading up to this event, and even the time period in the immediate aftermath, will be turbulent. I hope it won't be, but the implications of the super-advanced technology on the horizon are so vast that it's a fiction author's dream come true. The myriad of possible conflicts are rife for exploration, and that's what the *Post-Human* series does. Just as *Star Trek* is generally thought of as having a very positive view of science, humanity, and the future, yet there was conflict in every movie, episode, book, etc, the same is and will continue to be true of the *Post-Human* series. And just as in Star Trek, the humans won't give up because the technology presents challenges. They'll do what humanity has always done, which is persevere and hopefully overcome. The only difference is that Post-Human picks up where Star Trek had to leave off, since Star Trek is a franchise that was born before the implications of the acceleration of information technology were understood. Now that it's becoming clear that nanobots will end aging and lead to upgrades in intelligence and that we're going to merge with our computer technology sooner rather than later, a future in which humans still age, bald, and die doesn't seem to make sense anymore. But the positive spirit of that franchise lives on. I guess I'd say that, in a way, *Post-Human* is attempting to be the real *Star Trek* reboot.

Q. You say that it has become clear that nanobots will end aging, we'll upgrade our intelligence and merge with machines, but how do you respond to those people who'd argue that those technologies aren't on the horizon or are perhaps unlikely to ever be possible?

A. When I first had the idea for *Post-Human* and began writing it in February of 2005, some of technologies I was writing about might've been too far ahead of their time for a lot of people to understand. Luckily, it took me until 2009 to get it published and I wasn't able to Kindle Direct Publish it and reach a wider audience until early in 2012, so the technology the general public had been exposed to had time to catch up in the meantime. For instance, the post-humans in my books have an onboard mental computer called the mind's eye, and Google Glass could easily be said to be the first-gen version of this, so it's easy for new readers to accept that the mind's eye is the logical upgrade. Another example is that in the summer of 2012, I published a prequel that is now book 1 in the series, called *Sub-Human*, and I had one of the characters placed in suspended animation for more than a decade in a suspended animation body bag. When it appeared in the media that suspended animation was cleared for human trials earlier this spring, multiple readers posted links to the news articles on my Facebook and exclaimed their shock that a technology from my books was appearing in reality, as though it walked right out of the safety of fiction and plopped itself in the middle of real life. I wasn't surprised, however, as I'd only included suspended animation body bags in the book because I knew DARPA was really working on them, and I'd even watched a TED talk about it while doing my research for the novel. Basically what I'm saying is that the technology in the series, fantastic though much of it seems, is based in reality. In 2014, with Siri or Google Voice Search in most people's pockets, the general public seems to accept that AI is close at hand. With fingers and even organs being grown with stem cells, the idea that immortality will be achievable within decades doesn't stretch people's ability to believe or comprehend anymore. In short, the people have come a long way in just a very short time, and it's time for science fiction to reclaim its rightful place and get back out in front of the science reality. For the last ten years or so, too much sci-fi has been playing catch up, with the scientists and engineers leading the way while authors imagined end of the world scenarios that were arguably not even science fiction at all. Sci-fi authors have the opportunity now to do the research, understand transhumanism and the acceleration of information technology, and start inspiring the scientists and engineers of the future again.

****

35) *Longevity Cookbook* is Your Chance to Defeat Aging: Interview with Maria Konovalenko

The field of longevity science—also called life extension research or anti-aging science—seems to be everywhere in mainstream news these days. The transhumanist idea of conquering human death with science (and possibly even living indefinitely) is catching on. Everywhere, more and more people seem to be supporting the possibility of it.

One dashing 29-year-old scientist is helping to bring longevity research into people's houses—specifically into their kitchens. Maria Konovalenko is one of the lead organizers and authors of the forthcoming *Longevity Cookbook,* full of recipes and ideas that will help you live far longer.

Maria is studying biology of aging in a joint PhD program between University of Southern California and the Buck Institute, and has been involved in fighting aging for seven years now as a vice-president for the Science for Life Extension Foundation. Maria has a background in molecular biological physics, is one of the organizers of the Genetics of Aging and Longevity conference series, and is the Longevity Advisor of the Transhumanist Party. I had a chance to interview her, and here is our conversation below:

Q. Maria, what gave you the idea for a *Longevity Cookbook*?

A. For many years my team and I have been facing the same questions: What can we do to achieve a breakthrough in life extension? How can we accelerate the basic research on aging? How can we help as many people as possible live to see radical rejuvenation and life extension technologies invented?

The goal of longevity suggests two obvious lines of action. First of all, you need to utilize the existing knowledge and correct your lifestyle accordingly to live as long as possible.

Unfortunately, public access to scientific research on nutrition is quite limited and often hindered by pseudoscientific and unprofessional advice. In order to achieve some clarity we need to analyze hundreds of thousands of academic publications using modern bioinformatic methods. Secondly, you need to accelerate possible discoveries in life extension. This is a very hot topic at the moment, especially here in the San Francisco Bay Area, but the discussion is done in extremely generic terms. Meanwhile, society should know what kind of research needs to be done. A clear picture would undoubtedly broaden the scale of the vital scientific research.

We also noticed that the majority of radical life extension and immortality advocates adopted these ideas after reading books on relevant topics, and came to a logical conclusion that a book on life extension strategy would be highly relevant and much appreciated.

Q. What do you hope to accomplish with the book?

A. Firstly, we want to show everyone what should be done right now to live longer. Secondly, we strive to motivate people to live longer. Thirdly, we would like to expand the on-going research on aging ten-fold.

Q. Several commercial initiatives are working on the problem of aging. Should we rely on them?

A. We believe that the cure for aging can only be created as a result of a non-profit effort. This is an insanely complicated task that requires open data and a broad scientific discussion. A commercial venture cannot work this way. When money is king, all efforts are geared toward making more money. We, on the other hand, want to extend lifespan and improve health in the first place.

Q. Tell me about the others involved with creating the book?

A. There is Anna Kozlova, who is working in the field of organic chemistry. She is also a filmmaker.

There is also Anastasia Shubina, who is a genetic engineer, and she is also studying philosophy.

Steve Aoki has also recently joined our team. Being a superstar DJ and a talented musician and producer, Steve Aoki has a unique perspective on the future filled with innovation and technology, that he introduced in his album *Neon Future I* and in his latest release *Neon Future II*.

We are also working with remarkable scientists, and I think we will increase our scientific advisory board to 20 of the world's leading researchers. We will also need to attract designers, bioinformaticians, chefs, and specialists in motivation. *Longevity Cookbook* is a large-scale project.

Q. What is your favorite recipe in the book?

A. Speaking of food, I would prefer the diet that inhibits mTOR signaling and reduces inflammation. We will reveal what kind of food that is in the cookbook.

IF we are talking about the "recipe" of scientific research, then I love the idea of making the bacteria that live in our body act in favor of our longevity. We will talk in more detail about various scientific approaches to longevity in the book.

Q. The field of longevity seems to be exploding in popularity. Tell me your thoughts and where to do you see the field 10 or 15 years from now.

A. Well, it all depends on us. Our book is about that the idea of sitting and waiting, when science will do it all, is a pretty stupid idea. Longevity research needs support, and not only in PR, but primarily in money. A lot of money. It pretty much depends on what politicians we will elect – whether they will act in our interest for us to stay alive, or not.

If you want me to be some kind of medium and share a prophecy with you, then sure, I think in 15 years genetically modified stem cells and therapeutic cloning technologies will be a very hot topic. I'd like to highlight this one more time: how far technological progress moves forward depends on the people of power acting in favor of radical life extension.

Q. Maria, what is your main goal?

A. My goal is to make people live as long and as healthy as possible using the advances of science and technology.

****

36) Dr. Bertalan Mesko: A Medical Futurist Discusses Health and Transhumanism

It's an exciting time to be alive with so much incredible medical technology affecting our lives. As a transhumanist, I couldn't be happier about that fact. But understanding all that we can do to our bodies both now and in the future is complex business. I had a chance to catch up with Dr. Bertalan Mesko, and ask him to tell us about his new book, *My Health: Upgraded*, which covers the field of modern and futurist medicine. Mesko is a medical futurist with a PhD and MD in genomics from the University of Debrecen, Medical School and Health Science Center. His work has been covered broadly in major media.

Q. What made you write *My Health: Upgraded*?

A. I kept receiving amazing questions about the future of medicine after my talks. I wrote them down to understand the general public's interest in health technology and innovation better. When I realized that I had over 50 really exciting questions, it was time to answer them. That was my aim with

My Health: Upgraded. I firmly believe that it's time for humanity to step up and prepare for the technological revolution in healthcare. We must keep the human touch in medicine, and live healthier lives. Both goals are important, and neither should come at the expense of the other. In *My Health:Upgraded*, I present how I have upgraded my health in the last decade with innovative, but affordable technologies; and what the most exciting, important and alarming issues are when it comes to the future of medicine and healthcare.

Q. Who else is involved in creating the book? Who have you talked to while writing it?

A. I asked the opinion of visionaries such as Eric Topol, Ian Pearson or Lucien Engelen. I interviewed experts such as E-patient Dave deBronkart, Professor Robert Langer, Professor Anthony Atala, among others. I also asked companies to weigh in, from AliveCor and Withings to The Personalized Medicine Coalition, Intouch Health, MC10, Organovo, and Ekso Bionics. Their insights helped make the book as comprehensive and up-to-date as possible.

Q. How can we start upgrading our health today? Where would you start?

A. It's important to point out that buying devices is not the first step towards upgrading our health. First, we need to find what is wrong with our health, disease management or lifestyle. When I was a teenager I got fed up with the mood swings that every teenager suffers. One day you can happily focus on what's important, the other you are downbeat for no real reason. As a pretty rational person I decided to change that. But I needed data to do so. I started assigning a score between one and ten to my daily emotional, physical, and mental state in order to track changes over time. I thought it might reduce my mood swings. It worked. And I still log my ratings every day. Since July 21, 1997, I have not missed a single day. Early on I used simple notes. Now I save my data in a Google document. It takes me seconds a day. This way I can adjust my lifestyle whenever I notice trends, or a decline in the graph of my life. I found that my physical score is generally stable and high (meaning good) during the weekdays, my mental score declines over the weekend, and my emotional score is highest on Friday and Saturday. I further found a strong correlation between more exercise and mental performance - now I exercise every day so I can focus. Such a simple thing led to important consequences. The data helped me decide what to add or remove from my routine. It helped me live differently and find the balance that so many people are looking for.

Only after you know what to improve should you start looking for the right technology to help measure results. I published a video guide to help people find the best wearable for any purpose.

Q. Which technologies do you think will help the transhumanist movement now?

A. The majority of disrupting health technologies will help the transhumanist movement in the long run. But the two most interesting areas for transhumanists are health and disease.

In terms of monitoring health, the size of health trackers is decreasing fast and can measure more and more parameters from blood pressure to stress levels. The Japanese digital tattoo and similar thin electronics will make data collection even more seamless. Robots of micrometer size have been introduced to the general public in 2015. If they keep on shrinking, nanorobots could soon be living in our bloodstream as Ray Kurzweil has described.

Artificial intelligence algorithms could organize healthcare much better. As we start to understand how our neural system works, we might be able to upload information straight from our bodies. Martine Rothblatt brilliantly explained how such "cybertwins" would look like in her new book, *Virtually Human*. Such cyber minds would be algorithms having the same set of skills, thoughts and emotions we have.

There's reason to be excited for every transhumanist, but the challenge will be making technology safe to use, upholding individual privacy, and teaching the general public to accept and embrace the technology.

Q. What is the most heartbreaking / surprising story you uncovered while looking for the future of medicine that was about a "layperson" building technology to upgrade their health?

A. I'm always moved when I see examples of empowered patients taking matters into their own hands. In 2012 a boy was diagnosed with Duchenne Muscular Dystrophy. His father left his career in finance, relocated with his family from London to Massachusetts, put a team in place, raised seed capital and founded Solid, a biotech company with the purpose of finding a cure. There are literally hundreds of similar stories, proving that the future of medicine is not only created by physicians or researchers, but also by laypeople. And I'm always excited when laypeople design cutting edge technology to solve everyday problems, even though the tech in question has not been deemed "safe" yet. I'm talking about people who have implanted RFID chips under their skin to control laptops or garage doors and serve as a universal password to services and other devices. I should note that though sterile microchips are available online, we don't have long-term data about their safety.

One of the most exciting new areas for wearable technology is about literally upgrading how we think - how our brain functions. Should we start using these gadgets right away for getting feedback about how our brain works or are there things to consider and warnings to heed before we do?

When I want to relax I put on my Muse headband and open the related application on my smartphone. It guides me through the process of meditation. Then gives me feedback about how successful I was compared to myself before starting meditation.

For example, I have to think of as many members of a category such as cars, books, or movies as I can in one minute. This is how it measures my active brain. Then I can set the length of the session and begin. The beach sound alone can make me relaxed, but I really start focusing on the reward, which is bird song. I couldn't do anything with an EEG graph therefore I need such a device to translate my EEG into digestible results. The app tells me when my brain was active or calm. This is the only distinction it can make. I've been meditating with it for over a year. And I can see how calm I mentally am while relaxing. When I need to focus, I browse focusatwill.com and choose music types from lounge to up–tempo, which helps me focus for longer periods. Developers behind the freemium–based service checked the EEG signals of participants and filled the database only with the kind of music that supports focus. I switch to up–tempo when I need to work fast and to café creative when I need to come up with ideas.

Only a few ideas of what methods and devices are already available. What matters is we should be conscious about using them, and only use them when they are advantageous.

****

CHAPTER V: EARLY JOURNALISM

37) Discovering a Bush Tribe in the South Pacific

Searching for bush tribes sounds like something that belongs to an anthropological journal—or a Conrad novel. But Vanuatu is not your ordinary tourist destination. Most people don't even know where it is, let alone that it has some of the most traditional tribes in the world living in its jungles. This obscure nation, thrown like rocks across southwestern Oceania, consists of 80 islands--some inhabited, some not, some so shrouded with dense foliage that no one's sure. If you have determination, luck, and a lot of time, you may find something long forgotten on those islands that no one's sure about.

I was a seeker and my journey began years before when I set sail solo from Los Angeles, bound for the South Pacific on my twenty-five foot Pearson sloop, The Way. The first island I visited in Vanuatu was Tanna. I sailed into Resolution Bay and went ashore, finding the local chief. I asked him what he knew about isolated bush tribes in his country. He told me there weren't any in the south--but legend holds that deep in the north, far into its mountainous interiors, where the government had only surveyed by plane, a lost world might still exist. A place where adult men never grew over five feet; where money, monogamy, and a Judeo-Christian God were concepts never introduced; a people wild and raw, still in tune with the ancient heart of the Earth.

"But it's only a legend," the chief smiled, telling me. "No one knows if they really exist. Or how many there might be."

Legend or not, I was fascinated. I left Tanna and worked my way north through the island chain, asking more questions and gathering information at villages on the way.

In my fourth week, I finally hit upon something promising. I anchored off an island in a protected lagoon, adjacent to a tiny town, and started up a conversation with the local café owner. Soon I told him why I was in Vanuatu. With keen interest, he told me to come back the next morning. He was going to give me a ride to the other side of the island where he knew a boy who could take me to a remote village ten kilometers into the mountains.

"If anyone knows anything about the interior, the chief of that village will," the café owner told me.

The next day he drove me to the other end of the island. I was introduced to a teenager named Eritena, who was instructed to guide me to the remote village. The hike was three hours long, mostly up a large mountain. On top of it, with a superb view of the sea, eight thatched huts rested as they might've for centuries. A group of short black men wearing only loin clothes greeted us. Eritena introduced me to the chief and his sons. They invited me into a large communal hut where bare-chested women cooked at a fire. Eritena explained that I was in search of villages further into the highlands, that I was prepared to walk as far as necessary to find them. The chief and his sons, speaking one of the 113 different languages home to Vanuatu, talked amongst themselves for a minute, then explained they would take me into the interior tomorrow.

I spent the night in the communal hut, sleeping and eating on the ground with twenty other people, only thin mats woven from the Bandana tree between the dirt and us. I was awakened before dawn, a black bearded face a thousand years old shaking me. A woman carrying an infant suckling her nipple brought me a small meal of prawns and coconuts. Our journey began at daybreak. The chief and two of his young sons escorted me. The hike went on all day, across two swift rivers, over three rocky mountain ridges, through lush, untouched valleys. Sometimes there was a small path we followed, sometimes it disappeared entirely. On our final ridge, the chief stopped and pointed. I could barely see through the heavy rainforest mist, but in the distance eleven huts were built into a small clearing in the valley below.

When we reached the valley a group of men were waiting for us. These men were even shorter than the chief, their loin clothes made from the bark of a tree. They stared curiously at me for a long time, then hesitantly greeted me, first waving, next reaching out to touch my hand when I extended it for a shake. Soon they overcame their fears, though, and began crowding around me, poking at my white legs, pulling my bare chest hairs—the youngest gently trying to put his finger in my mouth to see if I had teeth like his. For a few moments, I was their experiment, confirmations of the same types of rumors they had heard about my "villages" as I had about theirs.

Eventually we proceeded to the village. I passed a group of women on the trail carrying firewood to their huts. They were topless, wearing only loins made with fresh green Bandana leaves. One of them dropped her load and ran behind a tree, frightened when she saw me. The men, already used to me, laughed. I followed my escort into the center of the village. From every direction bush people started appearing, gazing at me from afar at first, then moving in closer. When the high chief arrived, he was the only one not totally surprised to see a six-foot foreigner standing in his village. He walked up and warmly shook my hand with both of his when I offered it. He invited me into his hut and told his three wives to serve us food.

When I finished eating, he launched into a story. I understood none of the tribe's language, but from watching him point to himself and draw maps in the dirt, I figured that he had once, maybe twice, been to the sea, and perhaps even visited the small town. He called for his eldest son and pointed to his wrist. There was an old watch on it that no longer worked. The high chief took the watch, and using sign language, tried explaining to me that he had brought it back many years ago. I gathered from this and his other stories that he might've seen a foreigner before, just never in his village, which explains his people's great surprise for me.

The next day the high chief gave me a tour of his village. I saw many incredible things. The men at work used traditional tools: stone axes, carved wooden hoes, spears with sharpened bone tips. The women carried water to their huts in elaborately carved bowls, sewed dried coconut branches together to form roofs, cooked on open fires using banana leaves around taro roots as one would use aluminum foil around potatoes. The village had no material clothing, no steel nails for constructing huts, no idea what a small piece of paper with a face on it would be used for. The only things I saw that came from the outside world were machetes. And these I presumed were brought up from the settlements closer to the sea—the chief from the first village gave his to a young unmarried woman.

The following morning I needed to begin the journey back to my boat. I ate one last breakfast with the high chief, packed my backpack, and said good-bye. As I exited his hut, all the villagers were lined up, waiting for me. The high chief proudly walked towards his people and joined them. Moments later, the village burst out singing. The blending voices were so sublime a shiver overwhelmed me. I stood there slightly shaking, deeply honored, lost in time to a tribe as old and true as the earth I stood on.

The chief from the first village walked up and gently put his hand on my shoulder. He smiled, motioning for me to follow. We disappeared into the jungle, singing voices filling our hearts on the long journey home.

****

38) Does Landmark Unmanned Flight Spell Doom for Test Pilots?

Four weeks ago, on March 29, the X-43A, an experimental hypersonic aircraft hit a record velocity of 5,000 miles per hour (8,045 kilometers), more than seven times the speed of sound. It represented an aeronautical milestone.

The X-43A's unmanned flight also represented the growing trend in modern aviation to not use onboard test pilots. Unmanned aerial vehicles, or UAVs, are on the rise due to economics, pilot error, and concern for safety of onboard humans.

Dana Purifoy, one of NASA's top test pilots based in NASA s Dryden Flight Research Center at Edwards Air Force Base, in California, flew the B-52 bomber launch aircraft that carried the X-43A and its Pegasus booster rocket to its launch destination over the Pacific Ocean. Once Purifoy was 400 miles (644 kilometers) off the coast of southern California, he ignited the booster rocket which took the X-43A to 95,000 feet (29,000 meters), where it separated from the rocket and performed its record-breaking flight using its supersonic combustion scramjet.

"I'm not worried that just because the X-43A was unmanned it's a sign of things to come for the profession of test pilots," said Purifoy, who spends much of his time testing out experimental jet fighters for NASA. "Each aviation experiment is different, and human test pilots will likely always play be an integral part of many test flights into the future."

Almost 57 years after Chuck Yeager broke the sound barrier during his historic flight on the X-1 rocket plane at Muroc Army Air Field (now Edwards Air Force Base) test pilots are occasionally being replaced by computerized auto-pilots or radio controlled simulation systems when flying is deemed too dangerous for humans.

Some observers speculate whether earthbound telemetry rooms with data-reading engineers huddling around massive computers will someday make human test pilots obsolete.

The United States Armed Forces are beginning to test many new aircrafts that will be controlled remotely far from where the vehicles fly. In Iraq, America is already using over 10 types of UAVs for reconnaissance missions in hostile airspace. A favorite is the Army's Hunter, a short-range UAV with a wingspan of 28 feet (8.5 meters). It can transmit real time video images from the battlefield and looks little more than an oversized radio-controlled toy aircraft.

Another popular United States UAV is the Predator. The upgraded version, the Predator B: MQ-9 Hunter/Killer, went operational in the Balkans in April 2001. It can fly up to 50,000 feet and shoot laser guided missiles.

The Global Hawk is another type of UAV. "It's long range and can fly autonomously with preprogrammed computer instructions. It made its mark in aviation history when it crossed unmanned from the states to Australia a few years ago," said Janet R. Daly Bednarek, Associate professor at the history department at University of Dayton in Dayton, Ohio, who specializes in aviation.

Test pilots are quick to point out that even the development of UAVs will often require their hands-on expertise just to get these machines off the ground. Otherwise auto-pilot systems will be crashing themselves too often.

"There are just too many factors involved that a human pilot must test out in an experimental aircraft before many auto-pilot systems will work properly," said Commander Bill Reuter of NAVAIR s Patuxent River in Maryland. Reuter is the chief test pilot of VX-23, a squadron that handles developmental test and evaluation flights for Navy and Marine Corps strike aircraft, such as the F/A-18 Hornets and Super Hornets. "Test piloting is not a profession that is going to disappear with technology, but simply evolve with it."

For decades flight-testing included strapping humans inside experimental aircraft machines weighing up to 40,000 pounds (18,100 kilograms) then telling the pilots to spin and roll their planes out of control at 30,000 feet (9,150 meters) while traveling hundreds of miles an hour. Test pilots have to be physically tough enough to withstand up to 8 G-force, which is enough pressure on the human body to distort vision, breathing, and sometimes cause regurgitation.

Over the past 10 years, 23 United States Navy test pilots ejected from the cockpit during an emergency as they tried to save their lives. Four of them never made it. At air shows around the world where manufacturers sell their new planes, numerous test pilots have also been lost.

It's not only danger that threatens human test pilots; economics are also involved. Sometimes it's cheaper to buy a computer controlled auto-pilot system than to spend millions of dollars on building a suitable cockpit that can sustain human life. Keeping the human body happy while breaking the sound barrier at altitudes higher than Mt. Everest is no simple task; cockpits must be able to provide proper amounts of oxygen and warm enough temperatures for the human body.

Additionally, computers--in certain types of aviation experiments requiring precision flying--make fewer mistakes than even the best of humans. It's just another factor escalating the test pilots battle against machines.

Nearly 100 miles (160 kilometers) north of Los Angeles, in the Mohave Desert, the next generation of test pilots is adapting to new challenges. Edwards Air Force Base, named for Captain Glenn Edwards who died in June 1948 test piloting a YB-49 jet fighter, is the training ground for top pilots. Today s class is a varied mix of pilots and test engineer pilots refer to themselves as airborne scientists.

"If you want to be a test pilot these days, you need to be more than just good at flying. Many of the upcoming test pilots have several degrees in engineering and computer science," said Purifoy.

One way test pilots are sure to keep themselves in the loop is by working on new planes from design to testing to production. They no longer just listen to flight engineers, get in a plane, and perform tricks in the air as instructed.

"When not flying, today's test pilots are in front of computers, working on simulation systems, creating design plans and making sure the experimental aircraft will accomplish what it sets out to do when airborne," said Reuter. "I just can't imagine a future in aviation without human test pilots. They're indispensable to the whole process of getting experimental aircrafts flying."

****

39) For the Athens 2004 Olympic Games, Environmental Stakes are High

A sensitive coastal wetland and historical area 40 kilometers outside of Athens is being transformed by a massive construction project in preparation for the Greece 2004 summer Olympics. The Schinias Rowing and Canoeing Olympic Centre which consists of 2 man-made lakes of 2500 meters, spectator stands for 15,000 people, coffee shops, taverns, and a helicopter pad are being built upon marshland and a rare pine forest in the Schinias area of eastern Attica.

"It's an outrage," says Dimitris Karavelas, director of Greece's World Wide Fund for Nature (WWF), which is based in Athens.

The Schinias site hosts 176 species of birds many rare and endemic, one locally endemic fish species and one of Greece s three remaining Stone Pine forests on sand dune a priority habitat for the European Commission. Nothing should be allowed to be built there.

Greece s World Wide Fund, along with other environmental groups like Green Peace Greece, Society for the Protection of Nature, and Hellenic Ornithological Society have led opposition campaigns from the start of the construction. Their central aim was to convince the Athens 2004 Olympic development committee to move the venue to the more environmentally stable Lake Yliki, an already existing lake 75 kilometers from Athens. Their pleas were turned down and now the Schinias Olympic complex is nearly complete; the lakes have already successfully hosted a minor competition.

In the last 50 years, the area of Schinias has undergone numerous human pressures, including uncontrolled housing, booming tourism on nearby beaches, illegal land fills, and nearby farms hoarding spring water. All have contributed to the reduction of the marshlands and wildlife. Activities like motocross riding and the operation of a small civil airport have further tainted the area.

In addition to being a biodiversity haven, Schinias has a special place in history. Democracy was defended for the first time against the warring Persians by the Athenians in the Battle of Marathon in 490 BCE, which partially took place in the Schinias wetlands.

It's just another reason why the Olympic Rowing and Canoeing complex should not have been built there, says Irini Gratsia, an archeologist for The Hellenic Society for the Protection of the Environment and the Cultural Heritage who has fought against the building of the Schinias Olympic centre.

Excavations were not carried out in full and now that the artificial lakes are there, it may be impossible to find all the remains. In addition, think of the symbolic value of the place. Would the Americans build a stadium on their Gettysburg battlefield for the Atlanta Olympics?

In the Athens 2004 Olympic Committee headquarters, officials disagree with the NGOs.

"Archeological and environmental issues were carefully considered before the construction of the rowing and canoeing complex were built," says George Kazantzopoulos, Manager of the Environment Department for the organizing committee of the Athens 2004 Olympic Games.

"And we consider the area so important that in July 2001 the entire area was declared a national park—the Schinias Marathon National Park--giving far more protection to the area than there ever was before."

NGOs think the decree of the area a national park was lip-service and a way to ease the political hurdles with building in such an environmentally sensitive area.

When other national park gets created, dozens of workers and bulldozers don t start driving through it, creating a massive sporting venue complete with restaurants, a gas station, and mass-transportation means in a forest. That's not how protected areas are supposed to be treated. This decision sets a dangerous precedent for all Greece's other national parks.

Despite complaints by NGOs, the Athens 2004 Olympic Committee has made some positive changes in the Schinias area. Anti-fire measures in the form of sprinklers have been added to the stone pine forest, motocross riding has been stopped, and all construction has been outlawed (with the exception of the Olympic venue).

"Honestly, look at the some of the issues at hand," says Kazantzopolous. "There was an airport in the middle of the wetlands. We replaced it with two lakes that use the natural spring water from the Makaria Spring. In addition to making new ecosystems with the lakes, we diverted the spring water to the rare stone pine forest, which needed it since farmers in the area had increasingly been taking it all. Lastly, we are retaking measures to monitor tourism and protect the animals and plants. I think it's safe to say at the end of the Olympics, Schinias will be in better shape than when we first came."

****

40) The World Under Sail

It was a lifelong dream to buy a sailboat and take a voyage around the world. Even now I have memories of standing upon the edge of the ocean, vowing that someday I would see other lands and peoples, exposing myself to ideas and challenges far beyond my experience. In August of 1994, at the age of twenty-one, I bought a twenty-six foot Pearson Commander sloop, named *The Way*. Five weeks later, I left America to circumnavigate the world—and realize my dream.

When I look back on my life now, it seems to begin with that first dawn of solo sailing and the Los Angeles skyline fading into the morning sun. Those first moments are always the most frightening, yet precious. Since then I have sailed tens of thousands of miles, visiting 51 countries, crossing two oceans, and intersecting the equator four times. The first two years of my trip were spent almost entirely in the South Pacific, my favorite area in the world. From Los Angeles I made the grueling 2,400-mile/twenty-day passage to Hawaii. After a two-month stop in Oahu where I worked on my boat, received my diving certification, and surfed the infamous North Shore, I sailed 800-miles due south until reaching a tiny atoll named

Tabueran. This seven-mile strip of land that encircles a shallow turquoise lagoon was part of the Kiribati island chain. Here I spent the next six months of my voyage living among the indigenous people—Pacific islanders whose culture has yet to experience electricity, cars, hotels, airports, tourists, or Coca-Cola. The Tabueran people are a simple, loving community, living undisturbed today as they have for centuries before. One of the best parts about Tabueran was I didn't spend any money. In late November I sailed into its lagoon with $1,500 dollars, the amount of money I planned live on until I found work somewhere in the South Pacific. When I left in April, I had the exact same amount of money. I hadn't spent a cent; there simply wasn't anywhere to spend it. Yet my Tabueran island experience was priceless.

After leaving the Kiribati group, I sailed for another twenty days before reaching Western Samoa. There I saw the greatest fire dancers in the world perform for their people's Independence Day celebration. From Samoa, it was to Tonga, then Fiji. The age-old tradition in Fiji is to present a Kava root to the high chief of any island you visit. If he accepts it, he will allow you to stay on his island and protect you from any harm that comes your way. In the seven outer islands I visited in Fiji, I presented the Kava root every time. No harm ever came my way.

But after departing Fiji on a 500-mile passage to Vanuatu, I hit my first severe storm. For seventy hours I battled thirty-five foot seas, my sailboat being thrown around like a plastic bath toy. Perhaps I needed to present Kava to the Pacific Ocean, I thought. But soon enough Vanuatu came into sight and I pulled into Port Resolution for safety. After not sleeping for three days while fighting the storm, I dropped my anchor in the large bay and collapsed on my bed. I was out for 30 hours. I awoke in the middle of the night to drumbeats and a rumbling volcano less than a mile away. It was an errie feeling, but something I would soon get used to. Volcanoes and villager's drumbeats became a way of life as I slowly sailed through a thousand-mile archipelago that made up Vanuatu, the Solomon Islands, and

Papua New Guinea. The next three months of traveling would be the favorite of my seven years.

My most spectacular experience occurred on a large island in northern Vanuatu. I was one of the first foreigners ever to visit an obscure bush tribe deep in the mountainous jungle. Reaching the tribe involved a treacherous two-day hike across steep terrain and verdant rain forests. Twice I slipped down the muddy slopes, sliding like a skier who's fallen at high speeds on a steep icy grade. But the hike was worth it. On the final mountain ridge before we reached the village, my guide, a chief from another tribe, picked up a conch shell and blew into it. A resonating sound carried into the valley below. By the time we arrived in the village, all fifty bush people were waiting in a long line, singing a song to welcome me. It was a magic moment; the exact kind I dreamt of when I left on my sail trip.

I spent the next two days visiting with the villagers and closely watching their stone-age lifestyle. The high chief of the village had three wives, and his people never left my side, touching my blond hair and following me even on my visits to the jungle to relieve myself. The villagers had no material possessions, everything they used came from the jungle they lived in. When I showed them a dollar bill, they had no concept of it. My explanation of a thing called "snow" totally baffled them. Right before I left for the long hike back to my boat, the village lined up again and serenaded me. The high chief walked up and clutched my hand in a warm farewell. I was deeply touched and had to fight back my tears; the moment was simply too overwhelming, too special. As I began my journey back to the sea, the singing softly drifted behind me.

After Vanuatu I sailed to the Solomon Islands where I toured the battlefields of World War II, and later, while alone on my boat, fought my own war against Dengue Fever. In Papua New Guinea, I scaled some of the world's most active volcanoes and visited the infamous Mudmen in the Highlands. After a quick stop in Australia for some diving on the Great Barrier Reef, I made my way to Guam. Soon after arriving I got a job as an archeological salvage diver—otherwise known as a treasure hunter. For four months I worked on the recovery of a Spanish galleon that hit a reef and sank in 1690 of the southern tip of Guam. According to Spanish archives, the galleon was carrying a million silver coins. If found, the treasure would be valued at over $500 million dollars. The Pilar Project, as the excavation is called, is considered the most potentially lucrative underwater treasure hunt currently underway in the world today. Unfortunately, by the time I earned enough money to get sailing again, our team of divers still had not recovered anything more significant than cannon balls, pottery shards, and 33 silver coins.

From Guam I cruised *The Way* through Micronesia, learning the ancient types of sailing methods with locals in their dugout canoes. On some of the outer island atolls, only traditional dress was permitted. This meant that all persons--including women--must remain topless and wear only Lava-lavas. In Palau I spent weeks anchored in secluded coves amongst the infamous Rock Islands, home to some of the best scuba diving in the world. From there I left the Pacific Ocean and entered the Java Sea, making landfall in Bali--officially Southeast Asia. Bali is home to the rich Hindu culture and I visited numerous temples, many which overhang the rugged, vertical coastline similar to that of Oregon. From Bali I made my way to Borneo, where I took my boat up an obscure river, encountering traditional Muslim villages. Men walked around the bustling market squares with giant moon rings on their fingers and their multiple wives following attentively behind.

The Yellow Sea was my next major waterway, and not one I was fond of. It has the highest incidence of lighting and the heaviest amount of shipping per square mile in the world. Near Singapore I counted 456 freighters within sight, and a few days before Christmas, a radio station reported lighting occurring every six seconds for seven hours straight. When you travel with forty gallons of gasoline on board, nothing could be worse. On Christmas Eve I was on the VHF all night, begging for freighters to watch for my tiny vessel. I felt like an ant on a busy freeway. While my friends and family were at home safely enjoying the best holiday of the season, I was in a frantic state, more nervous than I'd ever been in my life. As if the shipping wasn't bad enough, a squall appeared on the horizon bringing lightning and torrential rain. My visibility was cut to less than a mile. Luckily, I was spared the fate of getting run down by a 400,000-ton monster with a propeller longer than *The Way*. Just as the sunrise was appearing I motored safely into the harbor at Singapore.

The island nation of Singapore was the ideal place to leave my boat to do some land traveling, and as soon as I found a harbor, I jumped on a train headed for Thailand. From Bangkok I flew to Japan and Hong Kong. An Australian model joined me for some of it. While trying to impress her in Macau, I lost a significant sum gambling in one of the world's most famous casinos. Funny now—but devastating to the budget back then. She laughed, making me dinner at her place and telling me of a giant bargain food store in downtown Singapore, similar to that of Costco.

The next week I stocked up there, preparing for the next phase of my voyage: a nearly straight shot across the Indian Ocean. Before leaving, a friend from *National Geographic*, Jennifer Hile, joined me on *The Way*. After motoring through the Straits of Malacca, we began a 1200-mile sail to what would become one of my favorite countries: Sri Lanka. Almost exclusively an all-Buddhist nation, Sri Lanka is country in disarray. People ride in hordes on the roofs of trains, snake charmers earn a living mesmerizing cobras, and locals discuss (over Ceylon tea) its ongoing multi-decade civil war. After three weeks of visiting the ancient monuments and world famous national parks, Jennifer and I sailed to the Maldives. Here there was nothing to do but surf, play the guitar, and spear lobster all day. Nineteen days after leaving the Maldives we reached Oman, the first of seven Middle Eastern countries we would visit. And still probably our favorite. What makes Oman different than the rest of the Middle East, is that the Sultan shares his oil wealth with his people, so that the standard of living for the average person is often similar to that of America. New cars and Rolex watches are a common sight. Yemen was another story altogether. Its main port, Aden, was filthy, dangerous, and mostly destroyed from years of civil war. Jennifer and I were in and out as quickly as possible.

150 miles from Aden on my twenty-sixth birthday, we got blasted into the Red Sea. The wind was howling forty knots from behind us. *The Way* made two record setting days until we reached Massawa, the main port for Eritrea. Reaching Africa was a great high. It was one of the original goals of my trip when I left Los Angeles years before. And Eritrea lived up to everything I hoped for—friendly people and an endless, dry landscape with stunning sunsets. The most startling feature about Eritrea was its lack of men my age. They have all been sent to the front, fighting the war against Ethiopia. Sadly, many never return. Nowhere was this more apparent than Asmara, the capital of Eritrea. Before Jennifer and I traveled there, we'd never seen a place with so many women, children, and elders—and no young men. Despite this tragedy, the people were some of the friendliest since the South Pacific. We were constantly invited to dinner and asked out for drinks by the locals. Eritrea has a number of brewing plants, and the local beer was both cheap and smooth to the taste. Jennifer and I had many wonderful late nights with the people we met.

From Eritrea we cruised along the coast of Sudan, finally reaching Egypt. Jennifer and I visited the pyramids, Cairo, and the temples of Luxor. After motoring through the Suez Canal, we sailed to Israel. Jerusalem is a fascinating city, and whether you are a Christian or not, I believe it's a must to visit. Something about the Old City and the impact it had on our civilization drummed very deep inside me. A great side trip we took was to Petra, in Jordan. Most people know it from the final scenes in *Indiana Jones: The Last Crusade*. It's even more amazing than the movie makes it. Jennifer and I wandered for days looking at the ancient city carved into rose-red cliffs.

My seven-year journey took me through three more countries: Cyprus, Turkey, and Greece—all of which have the flair of the warm, slow Mediterranean life. Every morning at anchorage I'd wake to herders taking their goats to the morning feed. After 10:30 AM it was ciesta time—too hot to do anything but sit in the shade, sip a cool drink, and watch the sea sparkle. Well, maybe play a game of checkers too, a Greek friend once told me with a grin.

My journey is over for now. Jennifer is back at work and I've left my boat safely on a tiny island in Peloponisia. But when I have the funds to return, I will make the sail home to America via the Atlantic Ocean. Great adventures in South America, the Caribbean, the Panama Canal, and the Galapagos Islands still wait. And perhaps I'll find in my final return to the states, that I just haven't seen enough yet, and well…maybe, I'll see the fading of the Los Angeles skyline into the morning sun all over again--the beginning of another dream.

****

41) Travel! Intrigue! Cannibals! Extreme Journalism at Far Ends of Earth

So you want to be an extreme journalist. You want to ride in rebel tanks, make first descents, shake hands with cannibals. What keeps your world spinning is making people gasp. It doesn't matter that you're 30, can't afford health insurance, and prefer to watch "The Killing Fields" over grabbing a beer with your mates. The 10,000 other more qualified reporters and their press cards be damned. This story, Kashmir, is the ONE.

Enter Srinigar. Walk past the gunner's nest of sandbags and barbed wire to the Broadway -- the journo hotel in town. An unarmed valet takes your bags.

He's one of the few uniformed persons you'll see for the next month not brandishing a gun. Inside your room you check under the bed, in the shower, behind the curtains. Nothing's safe until your eyes have scanned it.

After dinner, the tube goes on. A CNN correspondent is reporting on violence two miles from you -- but he's in goddamn Delhi. The remote hits the wall. It's sacrilege.

Next day. Rain. Lots of it. Your driver tapes a sheet of paper inside the window with the word "PRESS" scribbled onto it. Most militants can't read, but they know it means "TARGET."

You're on your way to Kargil -- visiting a bombed village. You arrive to people crying, children orphaned, roofs with fresh 10-foot holes in them. A 7-year-old girl points to an area in the hills where the soldiers opened fire. It looks like any other piece of dirt. Except it's the LoC (line of control). And it separates two Third World enemies with nuclear bombs pointing at each other.

You ask a villager if he's worried about a full-scale war. He's not. But he says you should be. Everybody knows China will side with Pakistan -- and America will side with democratic India. The question is who will Russia side with?

Hmmm.

A week later you're hitchhiking through the Kashmir Valley. It's safer than taking buses (think Israel). A Sikh with a blue turban stops his cargo truck. In you go. Speeding past are gunner vehicles -- Indian patrol units headed to the front. Soldiers stand alert with their fingers on M60 triggers. Many wear Mad Max motorcycle helmets, scaring the hell out of everyone.

The Indian military hate you. An occupying army always gets bad press. The gunners wave for you not to film. The officers refuse to be interviewed. The soldiers in the street turn their backs to your camera. It's no surprise the Indian Consulate General in San Francisco personally refused you a visa, forcing you to backdoor the process through Nepal. One day they'll find mass graves here and tourists will talk in whispers and click cameras at skulls.

Until then, the men with guns and helmets run the show. And every hour someone will continue to die or disappear in Kashmir.

A month later Pakistan is in sight. You're walking across Wagah, the only land border between the enemies. Sweat is streaking down your face. Confessions of torture victims, shots of military installations, proof of rampant human rights abuses burn a hole in your boots. The dummy copies are in your bags to be confiscated. But the customs guys aren't interested.

They're looking for a handout. You curse them in Hungarian with a smile and give them a folded $20.

From the border it's a b-line to the FedEx office in Islamabad. Tapes go off -- you get drunk in the Holiday Inn.

Enter Muzaffarabad, Azad Kashmir. Off the bus two tall men in Muslim gowns approach you. Get the hell away from me. Then you see badges. They drag you off to the police station. Are they for real or is this another Pakistan kidnapping? A few minutes later the police chief is frowning at your Indian passport stamp. You offer him money. He looks offended. You apologize. He offers you tea. You wonder if it's poisoned. Three glasses later you're off to a motel of his choice. He ends up liking you, but not trusting you. He wishes you a good night -- and slips in that the secret police will be following you everywhere.

Next day you go to a refugee camp. It's desperate, shocking. An old woman shows you her fingers; all 10 are broken in different ways. Younger women complain of multiple gang rapes by soldiers. Those husbands still alive turn away and cry. War is a frothing beast.

A week later you finally get access to the city hospital. Journos aren't allowed but the secret police you bought a carton of Marlboros for arrange it. Inside, it's a nightmare. Blood on the floor. Blood on the beds. Blood flowing from the freshly sawed-off limbs. The first five minutes of footage are useless. You're shaking the camera too much. When your nerves return you interview victims. One man with an orange beard says his 5-year-old grandchild brought in a timer-bomb dressed up to be a toy. Soldiers threw it into the yard while hiding behind bushes. It went off in the house, killing everyone -- his son, his daughter in law, his grandchild, his wife. Everyone but him.

Back in the states you suffer through television channels explaining your footage is intriguing -- but not for them. Too political. Not really an appropriate sell in this post-9/11 era. You push in "The Killing Fields" tape and scour the cabinets for whisky. Being home is worse than being there.

Until you read the paper the next week. There's a mention about Kurdistan.

About oil lords and genocide and armed rebels. You wonder if this story is a better sell. You wonder if you can pull it off. Yes, you think it can.

You're reaching to call your travel agent. You're hitchhiking in from Turkey. You're videoing Sadam's border. A Kurd gunner vehicle breaks through -- you're on it, Baghdad bound. The war has started. No permits. No questions. You're the first one in this far. You just need to make it out.

This is it -- this story is the ONE.

****

42) Becoming a Treasure Hunter

It must be every adventurer's dream. I sail into Guam on my sloop, *The Way*, finishing three years of island hopping and diving my way through the Pacific. I'm exhausted, unshaven, and reluctant but ready to find a job for a few months to refill my adventure purse. I didn't know what kind of work I was going to do, but I hoped it would center around my passion for the sea.

Wandering around a dive shop, I met a boat captain who asked if I knew how to scuba dive, because he was looking for an experienced diver to fill the final slot on an 8-man salvage team.

"What are you salvaging?"

"A shipwreck: the Nuestra Senora de Pilar Zaragosa y Santiago, to be exact. It's called the Pilar Project—off the southern end of Guam. Have you heard about it?"

"Sure," I said. "I've seen a Discovery Channel documentary on it. It's that recovery of a 16th century Spanish Galleon that was carrying enough silver—a billion dollar's worth—to build a city in the Philippines. It's one of the world's best known underwater treasure hunts."

David Tibbetts smiled. He was the captain of the Pilar Project's boat and dive team. "That's right, though technically, we call ourselves archaeological salvage divers. But since the mother load of over a million silver coins is still down there, calling it a treasure hunt is also true."

David explained what being a diver on the project required. He told me this wasn't the usual type of Club Med scuba activity. The project runs six, sometimes seven days a week. The team works off a rusty tugboat anchored near Cocos Island off Guam. Generally, everyone makes four or five dives a day, staying in the water as long as the dive computers and daylight allows them too. Only four months of the year (May through

August) at the wreck site are diveable. The rest of the months are too rough: already a two to three knot current rips through the search zone straight into the Marianna Trench. Most the underwater labor is physical and demanding.

Imagine working in a giant query, but 120 feet down. Often twice a day, a pair of divers will be required to lift the 110-pound anchors and relocate them a quarter-mile away. Other chores include clearing boulders and World War II debris, searching for silver with underwater metal detectors, and using the heavy underwater machinery: the eductor dredge. Sometimes one spends all day leading the visiting scientists or photographers around the places the team has dug. The biggest danger is getting bent. The biggest nuisance: camouflaged stone fish.

"But the visibility is great, right? So you can see everything clearly?" I asked David.

"Sure, often better than 100 feet. All the better to keep an eye out for the men-in-gray that like to swim around."

I cringed, remembering my love-hate relationship with sharks. I met a handful of locals in the Pacific with missing limbs from attacks.

David told me diving everyday would be strenuous, but that the crew and the dive gear were in excellent shape. "The team is filled with experienced divers and everyone tries their best to be safe, but, of course, the nature of the job, like being a fisherman in Alaska, is inherently dangerous." He titled his head down and began the story of how his good friend drowned on the project a few years back. The young man's air hadn't been turned on properly.

I listened carefully, and David's story transformed my vision of recovering giant silver bars and diamond studded treasures into that of a casket and an obscure Guamanian cemetery.

Still, ten-minutes later when I was offered the job, I took it. I knew there were risks. But the rewards outweighed them. Aside from the obvious benefits—diving every day and a sizable monthly paycheck to eliminate my credit card bills—there was the opportunity of being part of something historical. If the mother load was found, it's no bluff to say people all around the world could turn on the tv and catch the latest on the richest underwater treasure collection ever recovered.

Treasure hunting is not as obscure as it seems. Around the world, there are hundreds of ongoing projects—including volunteer and nonprofit ones—where travelers can join a treasure hunting adventure for a day or a year. In Northern California, there are ample private companies that will take you gold panning along rivers. In Israel, there are biblical archaeological digs where 2-weeks of fulltime participation is required. And in Cambodia, the nonprofit Earthwatch Institute has a program for adults to excavate ancient civilizations and their treasures.

Underwater treasure hunts are mostly limited to the hiring of professionals because of the diving dangers involved. But along with the dive crew on the Pilar Project, there were visiting geologists, historians, and private donors trying to piece together the puzzle of where the galleon might be buried. The area the Spanish archives pointed to was almost two miles long. So even a number of dive seasons might not bear much fruit—especially if, as many suspected, the coral had encrusted the galleon within itself.

"Nine feet!" a geologist yelled to me over the roar of the tugboat's diesel on my first day out to the diving site. I had asked him how much coral growth could occur since the galleon sank. "Over a 300-year period the Pilar could be a full nine feet into solid coral. And God knows how deep it could be into the sand. You guys got a lot of digging to do."

David drove the tugboat up to a buoy attached to the ocean floor by a thick rope. The swells were six feet and the trades were already ripping around nearby Cocos Island at twenty knots. The tugboat lurched uncomfortably; a rough open sea faced us to our West. We geared up and David turned on my air, instructing me on what we were going to do. He was going to be my dive partner for the first week, and today we were going to clear some boulders in an area where a cannon ball was found the year before.

I started putting on my fins, and he asked what I was doing.

"Getting ready for a dive."

"Not with your fins. We only use booties. And these…"

He reached into his dive crate and pulled out a weight belt with 30 pounds on it. I took it and struggled to strap it on myself.

He laughed, saying, "We work by walking on the bottom. In the next four months you won't put your fins on once. Think the moon, Zoltan."

Two minutes later we pushed off the ladder and speedily descended a 130 feet into the wide-open blue. I felt like superman dropping from a skyscraper—a kaleidoscope of ocean bottom colors shooting towards me.

As beautiful and exciting as my four months on the Pilar Project were, our team never recovered any silver. We did, however, find plenty of iron square-nails, pottery shards, and cobblestone rocks (thought to be the galleon's ballast). On one dive in our ninth week, David and I uncovered what was one of the finds of the season: three fully intact cannonballs. But the mother load of a million silver coins remained elusive. In late summer, weather forced the project to a halt until the following year. I parted company with my new friends and continued my sailing voyage towards the Philippines, thinking fondly of my time as a treasure hunter.

****

43) The X Factor: My Pirate Attack off Yemen

3:30 AM. Pitch black. My yacht eight miles off the coast of Yemen.

"What do you want?! What do you want?!"

Four men. No faces--masks. Their speedboat racing towards me.

"What do you want?! Money?! Dollars?!"

Pirates. Pointing AK 47s. Ramming my boat. Boarding.

"No, please! Stay off! I'll give you anything!"

The barrel of a machine gun. Five inches from my face. An Arab fingering the trigger.

"Please don't shoot! I can give you money, American dollars!" Frantic, shaking, my hands above my head.

"Cut! Cut! Cut! It's not working guys, it's just not working," the director interrupted, shouting. "Zoltan, you have to wave your hands and show more emotion or something, and Billy, you got to get that camera at a better angle. We're not filming the pirates' backs here. And driver, you need to bring the boat in from the west more, so that all the pirates can get their guns close to Zoltan's head. Now come on guys, let's take it from the top again. I don't want to be out here all night.

#####

200 yards off Venice Beach, Adrenaline Productions, contracted by the Travel Channel, recreated a pirate attack that my girlfriend and I survived last year. On an early January morning, Jennifer and I met up with the twenty-person production crew in Marina Del Ray. All the usual Hollywood

gusto was present: cameramen screeching up in Suburbans; directors crumpling scripts; producers sporting Ray-Bans; actors carrying props; sandwich boys to handle lunch. I sat down on the docks and answered interview questions about my experience, a Beta cam the size of a Great Dane rolling in front of me. But throughout the day, as different scenes and interviews were shot, finally culminating with the pirate attack, I kept returning to one thought: though the recreation for television may look accurate and realistic, there is no way to capture, no way to demonstrate, no way to relive what was the heaviest ten minutes of my life.

In 1994, when I had just turned twenty-one, I began my sailing journey solo on my twenty-five foot Pearson Commander sloop, *The Way*. I left Los Angeles and crossed 2,400 miles to Hawaii, spending years in the South and North Pacific before sailing to Southeast Asia. In Singapore, Jennifer came aboard and we worked our way through the Straights of Mallaca into the Sea of Bengal. Our first landfall after crossing the Indian Ocean was Salalah, Oman. From there we followed the Yemeni coastline for 500 miles to Aden.

To understand the intensity of the pirate incident is to understand my seven years of traveling before it. I wasn't your typical tourist--born to the wave of neatly packaged vacation tours--carrying two visa cards, a pocket guide to the best restaurants in the world, and a twelve-pack condom set. I don't call that traveling. For me, this wasn't the first, not even the second time a gun was pointed at my head during my adventures—which have included time in jail; crossing five civil wars; battling Malaria in the Solomon's; hitchhiking through Nicaragua; discovering a bush tribe in Vanuatu; crashing into a four-story tree while paragliding; barely surviving an emergency accent from seventy feet underwater when my dive tank malfunctioned on a treasure hunting job off Guam. And these things are nothing compared to the storms I've weathered alone a 1,000 miles from land on my twenty-five foot boat.

In short, I was anything but your typical bourgeoisie traveler. Still, nothing could prepare me for the enormity of the pirate experience. Unlike my other close calls, this one involved the X factor: Jennifer.

She was as much the all-American ideal as I wasn't. Young, blond, beautiful, graduated Cum Laude from UCLA. Walk into her parent's living room in Irvine, California, and you see two pictures. One of her as homecoming queen, one of Bill Clinton with his arm around her, holding a diet Coke—she used to work in the White House Press Office. That's the kind of girl I mean. So Jennifer met me in Singapore, selling her furniture and quitting her desk job as a researcher for *National Geographic*. She wanted to experience what she had been reading about for three years. Fine, I thought. We set off across the Indian Ocean; *The Way* chasing the sun, slicing through an electric blue sea.

Next we fell in love. The kind of love when you're in your late twenties, your genes are kicking in, you're dreaming about building a jungle hut together in Africa, saving the Rhinoceros from extinction, and home schooling your future child. That kind of love.

Then came the pirates. Now you see why two months later off the coast of Yemen I had such a harrowing experience. It wasn't just me anymore, but her. To make matters worse-- standing the late night watch through rough weather--my first thought when I saw four masked men approaching was of Jennifer's father. He's the VP of a high profile real estate company in Los Angeles.

"Yes, sir, I promise I'll take care of your daughter. With my life if I have to," I explained on a phone from a marina in Singapore.

"Good. Well Jennifer's mom and I feel safe then with her in your hands. She's our only child, you know—all we got."

#####

"What do want?! What do you want?!"

Their speedboat was approaching fast, but they were still too far away to hear me with their engine on.

"Jennifer! Jennifer, wake up!"

She woke up, asking from the bed what was wrong.

"Don't come outside! Hide yourself under the sheets and pillows! Four men in camouflage with machine guns are coming! I think they're pirates!"

"Pirates?"

"Yes, goddamn pirates! They got masks on!"

I threw my loaded flare gun behind me into the cockpit; it was useless against four AK 47s.

"Just hide yourself Jen! Throw the guitar and books over you! And keep silent! Whatever happens, we can't let them know you're here! If they find you, we're done for!"

The image of being tied up and gagged while watching her get gang raped flashed before my mind. My whole goal was to keep them off the boat. Not let them see a blond California girl. Give them as much money as they wanted. See if they'd settle for that and go away.

The pirates sped towards *The Way*, preparing to ram it. A spotlight attached to the their wheel house blinded me. When they struck, a deafening noise erupting from my hull. I was knocked of balance, falling into to the cockpit. I stood back up with my hands above my head; their AK 47s were pointed at me. The leader shouted out in Arabic to his man on the bow to get on my yacht. He tried to grab hold of my rigging, but the swells were violent, forcing him to be careful his hands didn't get crushed between the boats.

I called out, "What do you want?! I have money! Dollars! Dollars!"

If I could get the leader's attention away from his man boarding me, maybe he would call him off. But the leader only glanced at me, then turned to the man on the bow and began yelling at him. I can't be sure what he said, but I'd bet it was something about being an imbecile and *why the hell couldn't he get on the yacht?* The leader called to another pirate and told him to board too. The man threw his machine gun around his shoulder and ran to the bow of the boat. Just as they tried together to grab the rigging and jump on, *The Way* lurched sharply to its side, sliding down a ten foot breaking swell that crept up in the night. Everybody was knocked of balance. I crashed into the cockpit again. When I stood back up, the pirates' boat was eight feet from mine. The leader yelled at the driver to pull along side again.

"Dollars! I can give you dollars!" I started shouting frantically, making hand gestures that nobody had to board--that I could get it for him myself.

It took them thirty seconds to turn the boat around and pull along side. I continued shouting to the leader that I could get him money. I doubt he understood English, but after another wave broke over their transom, he reluctantly pointed with the barrel of his gun for me to go inside, saying, "Moonny! Moonny!"

I ran into the cabin and grabbed what was in my wallet. "Shit!" I cursed. All I had was a $50 bill. The rest was in Travelers Cheques. I thought about it for a second, then grabbed a carton of Marlboros and a bottle of Sri Lankan Whisky. I dashed out and precariously leaned over my guardrail, handing the leader everything. He let his gun fall to his side and took the items from me. Before he even looked at how much money I'd given, he curiously examined the bottle of whisky. Another set of swells came, pushing the pirates' boat further away from me. Twenty seconds later, the leader, satisfied, pointed for the driver to head for shore.

I ran down to hold Jennifer, collapsing on the bed. The next day she reminded me that alcohol was banned in Yemen. A thought that brought the first smile to my face since the attack. But there would be many more smiles on our journey together after the pirates, especially at her parent's home in Irvine watching the Travel Channel premier our documentary.

****

44) GREENING THE IRON CURTAIN

For 30 years, no one had seen an endangered Eurasian otter on the "death strip" in Lower Saxony, Northern Germany, part of the Iron Curtain that separated East and West Europe. From 1947 until 1991, the official end of the Cold War, land mines, barbed wire, and motion-sensing machine guns kept animals in, and people out. Then in the mid-90s, PhD student Liana Geidezis, studying otters along the former border, found the creatures spraint (urine) on the path tanks once busied. "I was so excited I jumped in my car and drove to the town of Salzedel--where I told the nearest nature agency the news.

A few years later, Germany's leading environmental organization, BUND, part of Friends of the Earth, offered her a job: to head the planet s most ambitious conservation project--a plan to green not just the German death strip, but the entire 7,000 mile former Iron Curtain that snakes across 11 countries. At the time the project was still in its infancy, but conservationists knew if the Iron Curtain went green, it would serve as the greatest symbol of a united Europe.

Today the task is still massive. Starting in the northern most point of the former Iron Curtain at the Barents Sea and finishing at its most southern end--the Adriatic--the belt of land that reaches 3,200 feet wide (1000 meters) weaves through towns and forests a green swath cutting a continent in half. Already it's being touted as the world's longest nature sanctuary.

"During the Cold War the safest place for wildlife was in the no-man's land," says Geidezis, aged 38. "Hunters, farmers, and developers all kept their distance. When the Iron Curtain fell, the Green Belt emerged with thriving wildlife and the best preserved habitats in all of Europe."

Starting in 1989, conservationists, mostly in Germany, painstakingly pieced the Green Belt together--sometimes purchasing the land outright using money from fundraising campaigns, sometimes begging their governments to donate it. In the last five years, BUND has collected over a million dollars from the public for private purchases of the Green Belt.

But 2003 was when everything came together. At the Perspectives of the Green Belt conference in Bonn, Germany s Environment Minister, Juergen Trittin, announced that the government s federally owned border land would be assigned to nature conservation. It was a defining and triumphant moment for the Green Belt and proof the project was possible.

The international movement, called Green Belt Europe, is a coalition of dozens of conservation groups, government agencies, and environmentalists, led by BUND. While Germany s 866-mile Green Belt is now 85% complete, 15% remains in the hand of privately held farmers who are reluctant to give up their lands.

With so many countries and agencies involved, bureaucratic red tape is another pesky problem that makes the Green Belt a tough sell.

Luckily, the May 1st, 2004 EU enlargement, where 10 countries will be joining the European Union, may change things. Geidezis hopes the EU membership will provide a shot in the arm for countries like Slovakia, Hungary, and Slovenia who are dragging their feet on what to do with their borders.

Any country joining the EU must adhere to strict environmental laws, specifically preservation of endangered habitats and wildlife. With over 100 different habitats and dozens of endangered animals in the Green Belt zones throughout Europe--like the red backed shrike, the black stork, and the fish otter new EU countries will be legally obliged to protect at least some of their green belts according the EU Habitats Directive, which forces members to protect certain threatened habitats.

But the EU enlargement is a two sided sword. New EU countries will receive friendly financial packages after they've joined--which in turn could translate into Autobahns and highways. It's going to be difficult to convince a government to commit to the Green Belt when they're not allowed to build a road through it.

In the end, the balance in favor of conservation may come from unlikely source: preserving history. Personalities like former Soviet leader Gorbachev--now the president of Green Cross International, a nonprofit conservation organization--are helping the Green Belt s cause by pushing for nature preservation in the former border zones combined with the build-out of tourist friendly cold war history sites, such as museums and memorials.

Such sites on the Green Belt and along the separate Berlin Wall are sprouting up--part of grand plan that state secretary of the German agriculture ministry, Stefan Baldus, speaking on the future of former Iron Curtain, said: is to combine conservation with history.

The Grenzland Museum, in Eichsfeld, Germany built partly inside a cold war 3-story watch tower is such an example. Only a 30-minute drive from Germany's Gottingen University, the museum showcases both "death strip" history, such as elevated helicopters and rusty World War II machine guns, and Green Belt photo displays of endangered wildlife and ecosystems.

"This two-punch combo is sure to benefit tourism in a big way," says Horst Dornieden, Grenzland Museum Director who has recently seen a spa center built across the street from his museum, part of the ever increasing tourism push associated with the Green Belt and Cold War history.

The hope is that tourism will bloom, adding financial incentive to the build-out and further protection of the Green Belt by governments and private citizens. So far the project runs through 18 national parks, including the 74,100 acre (30,000 hectare) Bavarian Forest National Park along southeastern Germany, named a UNESCO Biosphere, and its larger counterpart, the 70,000 hectare (172,900 acre) Sumova National Park in the Czech Republic, both which contain spruce and mixed mountain trees and altitudes over 3,000 feet. The Bavarian Forest received 2 million visitors in 2002, and is catered to by a variety of tour outfits. A network comprising 124 miles (200 kilometers) of bicycle routes, 49 miles (80 kilometers) of cross-country ski runs, and 186 miles (300 kilometers) of well-signposted hiking routes, gives visitors plenty to enjoy in the parks. Unique wildlife, including bison and lynx, also occupy the area.

The Iron Curtain has its roots tied to the end of World War II, but was hoisted fully by the 1947 Truman Doctrine a containment policy against communism. Thousands across Europe died or were wounded from land mines and gun fire by border troops as they tried to cross the former Iron Curtain to a free West.

Since 1990, the mines and the soldiers have disappeared, almost as if they were never there. Otters and other wildlife like wolves and bears come and go as they please. Locals in central Germany jog along old, worn-death strip paths. Tourists take photos of the former Iron Curtain watchtowers in the green Prague/Vienna route in the Czech Republic's Podyji National Park.

Geidezis thinks it may take 20 more years to complete the Green Belt. She warns success is not guaranteed if governments won't cooperate. But if tourists and wildlife enthusiasts have their way, month long treks and bike rides from top to bottom might become the quintessential European adventure and a potent pilgrimage along a most historic, green ground.

The only people blatantly opposed to the Green Belt are farmers, some who may have to give up their land to make way for wildlife preservation.

"But think about it," says Geidezis. "This is the most ready preserved habitat in all of Europe. And farmers want to give it up for sweet corn?"

******

45) The Mondavi of Pot

The heart of California's marijuana production, the "Emerald Triangle," consists of sleepy Mendocino, Humboldt and Trinity, the largest pot-producing counties in the U.S. A county-commissioned study suggested local economies in Mendocino are already two-thirds based on pot — with an estimated billion dollars in untaxed revenue.

Many people, including government members, say legalization is likely by the end of the decade.

"It will launch the birth of legal multi-billion dollar industry, that some think could one day overshadow the wine business, and make Napa Valley just a side trip on the way to the Emerald Triangle," said Aaron Smith, California policy director of the Marijuana Policy Project, based in Washington, D.C., which advocates the legalization of the drug.

Some real-estate agents suggest large tracts of bare land, good candidates for marijuana production, are poised to rise if legalization occurs, and are already on the mend, even as the rest of California real-estate slumps.

"Oh, this can go upwards. It's already up, despite the recession elsewhere," a real-estate agent at Ferndale Real Estate of Humboldt County, who asked his name not be used, fearing federal reprisals, said. "Clients often inquire about tracts of land up here and the feasibility of growing pot on them. Most of the best tracts are long gone. With legalization prospects constantly in the news, few land-owners would sell now, which naturally props up land values by diminishing the supply."

Agriculture land value has historically marched to a different beat than the rest of the economy since its value is closely correlated with the value of the crop grown on it, and the crop's price in the marketplace.

In the 1960s land in Napa county cost a few thousand dollars an acre. Californians considered it a backwater — not a Golden State gold mine. Now, even with the real-estate collapse, it's hard to find an acre of land in the wine region for less than a few hundred thousand dollars. Nearly 5 million tourists visit the area each year; only Disneyland has more tourists in the state.

Marijuana has some of the best profit margins of any cash crop. Pot plants can grow 10-20 feet tall, and one plant can produce as much as $5,000 worth of marijuana, at a street price of about $200 an ounce. By comparison, a single grape vine rarely can produce more than $100 of wine — and only after it's been processed and shelved for months, then shipped. Marijuana buds can be picked and shipped and smoked immediately.

"One main issue for growing marijuana commercially is the land zoning," Smith said. "When California does legalize pot, it's likely to at first be carefully regulated and controlled."

Some experts think special zoning will be required for commercially grown marijuana, as well as distinct water rights to protect connected farm lands and forests. The California Coastal Commission, which regulates property development near the Pacific coastline, likely will interfere with ambitions to grow as well, in an effort to protect the environment. Owning land that could commercially grow marijuana may not prove lucrative without proper permits.

Still, pot billionaires and hemp empires are expected to be forged after legalization. There will likely emerge a Robert Mondavi of the marijuana business. Agriculture companies will race to build marijuana harvesters, tractors and seeders. New pot-specific fertilizers and pesticides will be sought. Commercial development catering to hemp outfitters and smoke shops, like those in Amsterdam, will break ground and revitalize infrastructure. Counties will immediately see the benefits of increased tourism, which industry experts expect to surge in the region.

In 2005, a visiting professor of Economics at Harvard University, Dr. Jeffrey Miron, wrote a paper arguing that marijuana legalization could create more than $10 billion a year in the United States. Other experts have since agreed with him, and some suggest the amount is even higher.

"There will be a trickle down effect in everything, from real-estate value increases to new tax revenue," said Debbie Bills, who's worked for four years at a small hemp shop called the Hemp Connection, in Garberville, CA. "That could help us out of this recession."

****

CHAPTER VI: A COLLAGE OF WRITINGS

46) Sad News: My Dad Steven Gyurko has Died

Sad news. My Dad, Steven Gyurko, has died. He was 72 years old. He collapsed and passed away in his home. He had been unhealthy for a number of years due to heart attacks, diabetes, and aging, but he continued to enjoy his friends, family, grandkids, and watching news of my public career unfold. Thankfully, my Mom and him were inseparable, and she graciously took care of him for many years while his health worsened.

My parents had been married for 52 years and counting. The last time I saw my Dad in person he voted for me for US President in 2016 (*The Atlantic* recently ran a video with his voting in it). I had Face-timed a lot recently with my Dad, and my relationship with him was always good through the years. 18 months ago as I saw his health worsen, I offered to arrange and pay for cryonics for him, but while he wasn't religious, he simply did not want to do it. He chose to be cremated. He was, however, a great admirer of science, technology, transhumanism, and machines.

My Mom is pretty devastated, and she has come to live with me in San Francisco. She'll be helping my wife and I raise our kids. A bit of history: My Father and Mom escaped oppressive Communist Hungary in the middle of the night in 1968. I was born, a few years after my sister, in Los Angeles, California where my parents settled. My Father started a small plastics business that did well. For him and millions of other immigrants, the American Dream is very real, and thankfully, he realized it. He loved cars and dirt motorcycles, and the picture below is of my dad and I many years ago on an enduro motorcycle riding tour. My Father grew up quite poor on a small farm in Hungary, so it's been quite a journey for him to see all that has happened in the modern world.

I'm very proud of what my Dad did in life and how he did it. He was a dedicated family man and a strong-willed individual that lived life on his own terms. The last words I said to him were: "You did great." Also, two years ago I did a video interview of him via *Huff Post* that gives a good glimpse into his life: *http://www.huffingtonpost.com/zoltan-istvan/talktome-futurist-zoltan-_b_9879872.html*

I love you, Dad!

****

47) A Twitter Conversation Between Harvard University Center for Bioethics Faculty Member Dr. Louise Perkins King and Transhumanist Zoltan Istvan

April 4, 2020

@HMSbioethics (Harvard University Center for Bioethics): Transhumanism, libertarianism & calculating lives: Thoughtful #bioethics debate thread between @zoltan_istvan (Zoltan Istvan) and @hmsbioethicsvfaculty member @louise_p_king (Dr. Louise Perkins King):

@zoltan_istvan: Honest question: Are you willing to destroy 50% of US economy & reach 35-40% unemployment to save lives of 150,000 US citizens (mostly elders)? Pls assume it takes US economy 10 yrs for full recovery & #inequality grows. I'm curious of your answers 4 a #COVID—19 story I'm writing.

@louise_p_king: Not an honest question. As correctly pointed out above in many responses continuing our current efforts has better potential to save our economy. Reopening (which is alternative implied) will lead to 2-4 million deaths (up to 40 million) and complete collapse.

@zoltan_istvan: Hi, I disagree. I believe this will lessen possible life hours of all humans—& worsen inequality, steal personal freedoms, & kill economy. We should've been firm about quarantining only elderly & immuno-compromised people in Jan. & built ventilators then. (Link to Zoltan Istvan article on *Medium*): *A Letter About Coronavirus, the Longevity Movement, & Why Quarantining is Killing Us*

@louise_p_king: Most economists and epidemiologists disagree with you. What does isolation of those at risk look like btw? It's a massive number of people. Look at data from the south where mortality for 30-50 is 6 fold higher bc of poor underlying health related to poor access to care.

@zoltan_istvan: I understand your concerns & appreciate your insight, but I've done the math, weighed the stats, & consulted numerous medical people. I'm telling you & everyone else honestly, this is going to cost way more lives in the end (and quality life hours) by doing full quarantine.

@louise_p_king: You're wrong. I've cited analysis. Your cite is merely to ur opinion. State your numbers and analysis here. Btw we are not in "full quarantine." Define ur terms specifically how u calculate "quality life hours." Engage in this discussion with intellectual honesty.

@zoltan_istvan: My thinking/numbers are in my opinion *Medium* article I shared. Any move that doesn't act on the longevity (average possible life hours) of "all" humans currently alive isn't as effective. To protect a few, we're sacraficing the majority's overall longevity. Greater good is math.

@zoltan_istvan: FYI, this why you all could've used me at @HMSbioethics. It's not whether I'm right, bc I might not be. But I offer the other side (probably only scholar doing so), a challenge to see if my humanitarian argument (though brutal) might save more actual life in the long run.

@louise_p_king: I'm engaging here with you bc I want to understand your point of view. Your medium article simply states an opinion. There isn't enough there to truly address ur point of view.

@zoltan_istvan: 2-3 million deaths in US is most upper limit (mostly people near end of life). A depression also costs millions of lives. But my argument is to preserve $ for ending aging & disease. That's my math. Slow that research down even a year and humanity loses dramatically in long run.

@louise_p_king: 2-3 million is not upper limit. That only accounts for death from virus itself. Data from Italy and Spain show many more will die bc of collapse of health care and lack of providers.....

@zoltan_istvan: I'm seeing conflicting evidence of this (England, Germany, India less deaths last week?). & consider lack of driving, industrial & gun deaths right now). Also, your talking abt people w/ conditions (mostly older). My point is protecting biggest average life hours of "all" people

@zoltan_istvan: The only way I can statistically see my premise wrong is if the ultimate result of coronavirus is dramatically increased spending on science as a species or epic science innovation as a result of pandemic. Then near full quarantine is correct. But I doubt this will be the result.

@louise_p_king: Exactly. You've just proven my point. The effect of coronavirus will be dramatically increased if you let it run out of control and collapse the health care system ....

@louise_p_king: ...resulting in exponentially greater death rates not only from virus but from collapsed health care system and no one to care for those who fall ill from chronic or acute conditions.

@zoltan_istvan: I respect you but I think 40 million US deaths is so off that it's not realistic at all. But my anti-quarantine stance is humanitarian motivated; it's about lives & possible life hours. It's abt science research stalling, and costing the human race far more lives by 2035 overall.

@louise_p_king: Apologies for being misleading - 40 million is the worldwide estimate from Imperial College for coronavirus deaths. No one has an accurate estimate for how many would die in US but numbers would far exceed 2 million which only represents covid deaths.

@zoltan_istvan: Ok, thx; 40 million deaths worldwide is sadly possible. But bear in mind my premise. If anti-aging/medical research stalls just 3 years worth due to a Depression, the lives of 150 million r lost. This is a race to the future of curing disease. Every day of progress = 150000 lives

@louise_p_king: Where does this number come from? "Every day of progress = 150000 lives" and what if within that 40 million dead you lose a large number of the scientists that will push the innovations u hope for forward? I presume these scientists are from around the world.

@louise_p_king: What if the breakthrough innovation that allows for significant human longevity actually comes downstream from research into how to beat this virus? Or from fundamental clinical knowledge re delivery of care gained from fighting this virus?

@zoltan_istvan: Of course, all good points you make. These are tough times, & I have made my opinion known, but I could be wrong. Chance also plays a large part in who is right & wrong despite facts & logic, & there's no question your views are supported by the great majority of people over mine.

****

48) I Almost Died from a Leading American Killer: Choking on Food

I recently completed a European speaking tour discussing transhumanism, a social movement whose primary goal is to live as long as possible through science.

Ironically, I'll probably remember the month-long tour most for a specific 60 seconds—when I almost choked to death on thick, leathery bread in a German restaurant. This may be surprising, but the fourth-leading cause of unintentional death in America is asphyxiation from choking on food, according to the National Safety Council.

In fact, a few years ago, a high school friend of mine who was a talented athlete died when meat became lodged in his windpipe. In total, approximately 2,500 Americans perish every year from choking on food.

Most people never worry about the mechanics of how food travels from the mouth to the stomach—many of us have eaten tens of thousands of times without serious incident. But in today's modern society, with a range of new types of foods and textures, and the fact many of us are always in a rush (like I was constantly on my speaking tour), people should consider choking dangers far more. People should also know that they can choke on a wide variety of foods that accidentally get stuck in the trachea instead of going down the esophagus.

I never imagined I could choke on bread. However, European bread is different than American bread. It's much thicker, and when mixed with chewing and the mouth's saliva, it can become dough-like. I was sitting and talking with my family in a small restaurant in Wolfsburg, Germany, unconsciously eating thick-crusted bread before the meal arrived, when seconds later the contents in my mouth after a swallow had accidentally lodged in the entrance of my windpipe.

To compensate, I stood up and tried to take a big breath, but this only lodged it in further. It was then I knew I was in trouble, and now couldn't breathe at all. It happened so quick that my wife, sitting right across the table, didn't even realize I was choking.

Generally, when people choke, the Heimlich maneuver should be performed on them immediately. This maneuver is when you wrap your arms around someone from behind them, and quickly, powerfully lift up on their uppermost stomach, trying to force stuck food to come out of them.

But smaller people have a difficult time doing this on larger people. I'm 200 pounds and over 6 feet tall, and it requires serious strength to do the Heimlich maneuver properly on me. This ultimately means my physician wife, who is a third smaller than me, may not be able to help me from choking on food with the maneuver, even if she knows it well. She simply doesn't have the size or strength.

In my case, I was lucky that I was able to dislodge the bread from my trachea myself by standing up, jumping, and performing a version of the Heimlich maneuver on myself. But for about a minute I panicked as I simply couldn't get air into my body, and I was threatened with losing consciousness from doughy bread stuck just perfectly right in the wrong pipe.

People often die from choking on food because it takes so long to get oxygen back in their system. Sometimes, after passing out, choking victims must get a time-consuming ride to the hospital and even get a surgical procedure to dislodge edible objects. First-responding paramedics can't necessarily dislodge the food themselves even with emergency breathing tubes, and so it often has to be done in the emergency room by doctors.

Even in a major city near medical services, this process can take 15, or even 30, minutes before air finally makes its way back into one's body. It's quite easy to die within that period. And even if someone is brought back to consciousness, choking victims may have suffered permanent and debilitating damage from lack of oxygen to organs, including severe brain damage.

Here are three simple rules for avoiding one of America's leading killers. First: Don't underestimate the dangers of eating, and always chew your food well. Get used to taking smaller bites and making smaller swallows as a lifetime habit.

Two: Many types of foods can cause you to choke—it's not just meat. Don't be fooled by foods you think are safe, like bread, carrots, and peanut butter.

Three: Know and occasionally practice the Heimlich maneuver so you can help others and even yourself in an emergency.

****

49) Interview with my Mom, Ilona Gyurko

At the time of this brief video interview in San Francisco, Ilona Gyurko was 75 years old. She had recently starred in the feature documentary of her son's life IMMORTALITY OR BUST. She was married to Zoltan Istvan's father (Steven Gyurko, aka Apuci) for 53 years.

Zoltan: Why did you raise me a Catholic and give me a Catholic background?

Ilona: Well, at that time, I thought that was the best thing and would give you the best education.

Zoltan: What do you think overall of your life, coming to America from Hungary?

Ilona: I really believe I had a very happy life. I often think about it: I believe I'm not regretting anything.

Zoltan: One of the interesting things about Apuci was his perspective on business at the end of his life. What did you think about the economic opportunities when you got to America compared to Hungary?

Ilona: Oh, the opportunities were overwhelming in America. And we took very good advantage of them. And I think partially that's why my life is really good right now, because we worked hard, and earned hard. I had everything—almost everything—that I ever wanted in my life.

Zoltan: What do you think about how much change has occurred from when you first left Hungary to now? I mean technological, social, and cultural change? For example, earlier we were talking about house prices being $3 million dollars in my neighborhood.

Ilona: Oh, that's amazing, and I used to be sorry for my kids, because when I was younger, I was worried that they'd never be able to achieve the success to buy a home. But apparently, I was wrong. They reached as far as they could, and they learned from the parents to do good and try hard.

Zoltan: What do you think is the state of America and democracy right now, because of course when you left Hungary it was a Communist regime. And you came to free America, but it's also a bit crazy, especially now?

Ilona: I think even if everyone thinks it's crazy in America, life is still good here—much better than most countries all around the world. And as much as everyone is moaning and bitching about how things are here, I believe it's not as bad as they are thinking about it.

****

50) Quotes and Reactions from my Wife, Dr. Lisa Memmel

Zoltan Istvan's wife, Dr. Lisa Memmel, has made numerous interviews during her husband's political campaigns, including for his Immortality Bus adventure across the country. Here are four questions she answered for media (while holding Isla, their new baby in her arms) as Zoltan readied the bus for departure:

Journalist: Please tell us what it's been like having the bus in your front yard the past couple weeks?

Lisa: I think we've definitely been the talk of the street, and Zolt was a little bit frustrated for the first day or two because everybody kept stopping over and wanting to know what the bus was for. People wanted to have a tour of the inside and wanted to talk about it all, and of course that made it bit difficult for Zolt to get anything done since he had to do days of construction work to transform it into a giant coffin. I think it's been very amusing to our neighbors.

Journalist: When he told you that he wanted to run for President, what was your first reaction when you heard that?

Lisa: I was a little bit surprised, but I wouldn't put something like that past him. I was also a little surprised when he told me about the idea of the coffin bus, and I was a little bit dubious that it would all happen, but indeed it has happened *(Lisa looking toward the bus laughing)*…so there we are.

Journalist: What has been your contribution to the to the Immortality Bus?

Lisa: I've contributed a lot of pots of coffee and a lot of moral support.

Journalist: You're a doctor, right? And so how do you position yourself with the idea of immortality? And how is this idea to you as a scientist, or you know, a medical person?

Lisa: Well, I'm an obstetrician/gynecologist, so I can't talk about the neuroscience or talk about the future. I unfortunately only know my specialty, so I can talk about babies being born and all that. But I'll leave the rest to Zolt and to experts.

###

Dr. Lisa Memmel plays an important supporting role in the feature documentary IMMORTALITY OR BUST now on Amazon Prime. Here are some of those interviews that appear in the documentary.

Director Daniel Sollinger: How did you and Zoltan meet?

Lisa: Zoltan and I met on Match.com. I used to do a lot of traveling in my younger years, and I think the thing that drew me to him and his profile is that he loved traveling, that he led such a fascinating life—that he was such an interesting person. And the fact that he was with *National Geographic* for years, and that he traveled to over 100 countries, that I just felt like I had to meet him.

Director Daniel Sollinger: What do you think of Zoltan wanting to live forever via science?

Lisa: At first in our relationship, when Zoltan started talking about wanting to live forever and talking about the transhumanism thing, I was incredibly skeptical—as I still somewhat am. Even though I'm skeptical, I'm still supportive. After all, technology is advancing at incredible speeds, and who knows what could happen in our lifetimes?

Director Daniel Sollinger? How did Zoltan tell you he was going to run for President?

Lisa: I think he actually wrote a note to himself, and put it on the refrigerator, and that was to remind him not to have a midnight snack, because he was trying to lose wight. So he wrote this note to himself saying "I'm going to run for President", and he taped it up on the fridge door. I woke up the next morning, and when I saw the note, I asked: "What is this? You want to run for President?" And he was like: "Yeah, don't you think it's a brilliant idea? Do you think I'd be a great President? I'm going to run for President."

****

51) Poem: *Death*

Sad
fate alone
brought you here
on darkest of paths.

Use these wings of lead
to view the vast nigresence
with no sympathy of life about

Witness drab cloudy windows
where horrible drownings occur
the remnants of these deaths
no longer lead to sticky births

Terrible spectator of loss
crash into a fresh grave
you dug so long ago

Bury yourself well
dirt on smarting
ugly wounds
end in pain

****

52) Song: *The Anti-You*

I saw you
Did you see me
Rising through your excess
Bearing pangs of eternity

An angry child
A protégée
One who would not believe
like the other lambs you breed

Chorus
I am the anti-you
I am the anti-you
I'm hoping to kill you
I am the anti-you

Others are fools
Lives with nothing to save
Squandered uses and dreams
Let them eat their cakes in the grave

I am the acid man
Stealing the fire from home
My evolution rapes your pride
You're not the only one who loves life

Chorus
I am the anti-you
I am the anti-you
I'm hoping to kill you
I am the anti-you

Guitar riff

Chorus
I am the anti-you
I am the anti-you
I'm hoping to kill you
I am the anti-you

****

53) Cato Institute's *Cato Unbound* Debate: A Rebuttal: Deniers and Critics of AI Will Only Be Left Behind

Professor David D. Friedman sweeps aside my belief that religion may well dictate the development of AI and other radical transhumanist tech in the future. However, at the core of a broad swath of American society lies a fearful luddite tradition. Americans—including the U.S. Congress, where every member is religious—often base their life philosophies and work ethics on their faiths. Furthermore, a recent Pew study showed 7 in 10 Americans were worried about technology in people's bodies and brains, even if it offered health benefits.

It rarely matters what point in American history innovation has come out. Anesthesia, vaccines, stem cells, and other breakthroughs have historically all battled to survive under pressure from conservatives and Christians. I believe that if formal religion had not impeded our natural secular progress as a nation over the last 250 years, we would have been much further along in terms of human evolution. Instead of discussing and arguing about our coming transhumanist future, we'd be living in it.

Our modern-day battle with genetic editing and whether our government will allow unhindered research of it is proof we are still somewhere between the Stone Age and the AI Age. Thankfully, China and Russia are forcing the issue, since one thing worse than denying Americans their religion is denying them the right to claim the United States is the greatest, most powerful nation in the world.

A general theme of government regulation in American science is to rescind red tape and avoid religious disagreement when deemed necessary to remain the strongest nation. As unwritten national policy, we broadly don't engage science to change the human species for the better. If you doubt this, just try to remember the science topics discussed between Trump and Clinton in the last televised presidential debates. Don't remember any? No one else does either, because mainstream politicians regretfully don't talk about science or take it seriously.

But AI is a different political and philosophical dilemma altogether. AI is potentially the Holy Grail of all inventions, and it will bear the seeds of our own morals, idiosyncrasies, and prejudices. Rachel Lomasky and Ryan Calo in their articles may declare that Hanson Robot and Saudi Arabian citizen Sophia is a fake, but make no mistake: Fakeness (or semi-hyperbole) is more and more how the stealthy modern world moves forward. Just look who is sitting in the White House—arguably the world's most accomplished living newsmaker. For most practical purposes, it's irrelevant whether that news is fake or real. All that matters that is it's effective enough—and budgets get created around it.

Sophia is also effective. Instead of seeing her as unfortunate affront to the conversation of robot rights because she is not yet truly intelligent—as some of my other April 2018 Cato Unbound contributors seem to believe—I think we ought to see her as the beginning of our greatest and perhaps most important invention—one for humanity that will pave the way for the millions of smart AIs that are likely to come after her (or even directly from her).

Science and technological innovation are dictated by the scientific method. This is the idea that no one is ever right, but statistical probability can become more and more certain via successful repetitive testing, to the point that we can plan manned missions to Mars and know we'll likely succeed without ever having done it before. We have the intelligence to believe in almost anything—especially if we can test it. Sophia is part of our journey in a changing intellectual landscape of humans becoming more than biological beings—through rigorous testing of all that she is technically, philosophically, and culturally to us.

Saudi Arabia—like Trump—is correct to jump on the opportunity to embellish and parade its perspectives and national ambitions. As global citizens, we have the choice to take it seriously or not. But we don't have the choice to deny it, because we will only be left behind.

Progress is rarely welcomed or appreciated by society when it first happens. Visionaries get burned at the stake, or in modern times sued, fired from companies they created, and blackballed from media. But over time, ideas that are transformative survive, and on occasion, change the world. It may not be that Sophia definitely changes the world, but an AI like her soon will. We ought to be very careful to listen objectively and strive to shape AI—no matter how simple or empty of a shell our thinking machines seem now. We are listening to the birthing pangs of a new intelligence that almost certainly will make our own obsolete long before this century is out.

****

54) Remarks on my Novel *The Transhumanist Wager*

When I set out to write *The Transhumanist Wager* five years ago, I did not intend it to become an edgy, controversial book. For much of my adult life, I have been a journalist covering environmental, wildlife, and human rights stories. My articles and television episodes—many for the National Geographic Channel—were welcomed in any culture and in any country. My stories were the type that a family could amicably discuss over the dinner table, or watch on television while happily cuddling together on a couch.

Perhaps it was the effect of the war zones I covered as a journalist, but *The Transhumanist Wager* soon took on much more contentious ideas of human endeavor and culture. For a human being, most conflict zones highlight a simple fact: Once presented with horror and death, one tends to quickly discover degrees of emotion and experience never imagined or thought possible before. For me and the difficult moments that I still vividly remember, those incidents gave me the powerful conviction that human life should be preserved indefinitely, at any cost.

Jethro Knights, the main protagonist in my novel, also realizes this early in his life, after almost stepping on a landmine in a war zone (a similar incident happened to me in Vietnam's DMZ while filming a story on bomb diggers). The revelation for Jethro is so sharp, so penetrating, so intense that nothing will ever be the same for him again.

It is from this vantage point that *The Transhumanist Wager* was written. And it is from the landmine experience that Jethro discovers the mortality crisis not only in himself, but in every human being alive. That crisis takes on the form of a wager—a choice that every human must make in the 21st Century: to die eventually; or to try to live indefinitely. And if we try to live indefinitely, then we should use every tool and resource of science and technology available to us, Jethro insists. And we should do it immediately.

This is the quintessential message of *The Transhumanist Wager*—as well as my own message to the world as an author and philosopher. A rational and scientific-minded society owes itself the strictest dedication to applying its resources and minds to overcoming that which has been the greatest downfall of our species: our mortality.

The Transhumanist Wager presents an original, comprehensive, and rational new philosophy called TEF, or Teleological Egocentric Functionalism.

TEF is predicated on logic, a simple wager that every human faces:

> *If a reasoning human being loves and values life, they will want to live as long as possible—the desire to be immortal. Nevertheless, it's impossible to know if they're going to be immortal once they die. To do nothing doesn't help the odds of attaining immortality—since it seems evident that everyone will die someday and possibly cease to exist. To try to do something scientifically constructive towards ensuring immortality beforehand is the most logical conclusion.*

While most people around the world may believe that human immortality is still centuries off or impossible to accomplish without divine intervention, researchers in the life extension and human enhancement fields know we are only decades away from scientifically achieving individual ongoing sentience.

Irrespective of nationality, culture, heritage, religion, and all social interaction, TEF insists that the most important and urgent goal for any human being is to secure immortality--even if the attainment of that goal means the fundamental transformation of the individual into something nonhuman. TEF also insists that the most important and urgent goal for society is to work towards ending death for the individual.

Such unprecedented change for human beings and civilization would inevitably mean a paradigm shift for our species. Because a vast majority of people around the world are guided by archaic religions, unrefined cultures, and irrational reasoning, most humans and their governments will initially oppose such advancements. TEF sees any opposition that directly interferes with a transhumanist's attainment of ongoing sentience as a violation of essential freedoms, as an unwarranted act of aggression, and as criminal manslaughter. TEF believes transhumanists must protect their goals via any means necessary.

Beyond the imperative of attaining immortality, TEF has created the Three Laws of Transhumanism to help individuals efficiently navigate the future.

1) A transhumanist must safeguard one's own existence above all else.

2) A transhumanist must strive to achieve omnipotence as expediently as possible—so long as one's actions do not conflict with the First Law.

3) A transhumanist must safeguard value in the universe—so long as one's actions do not conflict with the First and Second Laws.

These laws provide clarity for long term transhuman ambitions and dominate TEF's ethical, metaphysical, and epistemological outlooks. Through them, TEF establishes a broad, concrete framework for transhumanists to successfully evolve into the most advanced entities they can become, which is their ultimate goal.

****

55) Stop Impersonating me on Senior Dating Sites, Donating Fake Twitter Followers to My Presidential Campaign, and Vandalizing my Wikipedia Page

Being in the limelight sucks. It's not that I'm really popular in the Justin Bieber kind-of-way, but in the last few years I've managed to show up a lot in the media, talking transhumanism, technology, and futurist issues. Thankfully, most of the coverage I've received has to do with my ideas and writing, and more recently, my 2016 US Presidential campaign for the Transhumanist Party.

Lately, however, I've also seen the darker sides of being in the spotlight, sides that seem dangerous, dishonorable, and outright ridiculous. The truth is that much modern media has become a circus, and large portions of it can no longer be trusted.

I don't remember it always being like this. I had the luck of becoming a journalist for the National Geographic Channel in my 20s. For a few years I worked with legendary editor John Stickney at *The New York Times Syndicate,* which put our National Geographic articles through its wire service. It was the best of both worlds--editors from the *New York Times* and National Geographic cowered over my stories. On one hand, it was very difficult, because every fact in a story had to be correct and double checked. On the other hand, it was great learning, because I understood that if a story didn't check out, no matter how good it was, it didn't run--I don't care if you were announcing the Pope had a lover.

Fast-forward to today, and journalism is not always the same. Some sites blend the lines between sensational ideas and solid facts. Sometimes these stories are great, and other times they are far more than questionable. Of course, social media does the same thing. And, frankly, most of us get our information and news from social media these days. And we make quick judgements about that media based on social media shares the amount of likes or followers someone has who is sharing the story.

A system like this is rife with abuse.

I never really cared about it until I was thrust into the spotlight. Then all of a sudden, the darkness bacame apparent. Most the abuse in my case has been in the form of sabatoge. For example, people on Wikipedia have been editing out obvious facts from my Wikipedia page, putting headline tags that question the legitimacy of the page, or the authors of it. Last month, almost half of the page disappeared and has not returned. Unfortunately, many journalists (shame on you!) use Wikipedia to quickly get information for stories. But what they don't read is the history of the page itself, where the truth can often be discerned. For example, detractors don't want to credit me with having written in *Wired UK*, even though an article there was one of my most popular stories, and articles from the *National Review* to *PJ Media* wrote commentaries on it. They also are trying to merge the Three Laws of Transhumanism page into another, saying it doesn't deserve a stand-alone page, ever though it's in dozens of articles and the laws are being taught in colleges across the country now.

Okay, Wikipedia is forgivable. But the other day some lady asked me why I was stalking her on an age 50 an over website. I told her I'm a presidential candidate, happily married with two kids, and am only 42 years old--It's obviously not me. She then proceeded to tell me someone was using my identity to pick up women on a senior dating site, and that upon further research they had a history of complaints from women. Sigh. I advised her to contact the police about it. I get a 100 messages a day. I can't answer everyone anymore.

But it's not always people doing something wrong against me. The other day, on April 21st, I had a respectable 17,200 followers on twitter. I know from following my account that about 10 people a day follow me. Once, when I was on the Joe Rogan Experience, about 800 people followed me in a few hours. Later that day, though, I had 21,500 followers. What the hell, I thought? Someone is either sabatoging me or supporting me--both which are unacceptable. A day later, I received an email on facebook telling me to "enjoy" my new 4000 followers, courtesy of a supporter.

I answered: Are you kidding me? I have reputation to protect, including editors that follow me. This is a PR nightmare to get fake followers.

This so-called supporter then went and on and on telling me that 90% of celebrities have fake followers. I don't follow celebrities or have TV so I was unaware of that. I researched it and realized he might be right, and that ge meant the best for me and my campaign. Nonetheless, I have editors and judicious people that follow me, and adding fake twitter followers is in such bad taste that I unfriended the person on Facebook.

It does however bring up a perfect metaphor of the modern-day media problem we all face: truth in the face of instantaneous web traffic where everyone has some voice--and buying that voice is simple and cheap. For example, did people donate twitter followers to Obama? My mom offered to buy me some Facebook friends for Xmas.

My response was simple, "Can they vote too, Mom?"

It reminds me about Ted Cruz, who paid 10,000 students to hear his opening speech. Or Putin who bussed in paid people to make his rallies seem bigger.

Laws should probably be made against this stuff. Our perception of reality, which is increasingly dominated by online media, is at stake. Otherwise we won't see the forest through the trees. And our perception of reality and understanding will be very damaging.

****

56) On Culture's Humanicide

In my novel, *The Transhumanist Wager*, I talk specifically about a strange concept: how our societies and their cultures are effectively snatching away our productive and potential life hours by allowing death to overcome and "kill" us. I label this *humanicide*. In fact, I go so far as to say that when government, religion, heritage, media, or any other organization or social force systematically deters science and technology from eliminating aging and death, citizens should be calling this act: *criminal manslaughter*. In a world where scientists are only decades away from achieving an ongoing sentience for individual human beings, criminal manslaughter is a fitting legal term.

And like all other crimes, criminal manslaughter needs to be addressed by legal means and criminal prosecution. It's my hope that groups around the world will try to form non-profit *transhuman-minded legal teams* to go after and prosecute organizations, cultural bodies, and government entities that systematically try to make society and its people believe that "death is okay." These new legal teams should attempt to prosecute anyone that deliberately promotes agendas and actions that prematurely end people's lives. Death is not okay. And every time someone or some group spends resources on donations for religion instead of donations for science, or our governments spend trillions of dollars on wars instead of trillions of dollars on the war on cancer, or citizens accept an anti-science culture instead of a pro-science culture, then they are committing an incompetent and wrong deed. A deed that leads to the premature end of each one of your lives—and each of your loved one's lives.

This is a matter of the most serious consequence. For transhumanists, indefinite lifespans are everything. And we are on the cusp of achieving it. Together, we must construct a culture that believes and wants this amazing opportunity of unlimited longevity. In the future, I see transhuman legal teams actively striving to criminally prosecute and legally harass all organizations that promote a culture of human death as being desirable. We should not tolerate anyone standing in the way of our species march to individual immortality via science and technology. Anyone that supports philosophies that prematurely end human lives should be warned that they can be prosecuted and hassled for such irrational malice—that they can be dragged through court, forced to spend money on lawyers, and possibly put into prison. We must put the Vatican and evangelical churches around the world on notice. We must put mass media and big business on notice. We must put the U.S. Congress, the White House, and international governments on notice. I am finished with anyone or anything stealing years of my life for their inane causes and erroneous ideas. I hope you are too. In a world where scientists and technologists are arguably only twenty-five years away from achieving ongoing sentience for the human being, anti-life/pro-death attitudes and policies are now unacceptable.

Feel free to reach out to me with more ideas. Feel free to repost this letter anywhere you like. I would be happy to help organize these legal teams and their agendas on where best we could make a lasting impact to preserve our lives and eliminate death for our species.

Yours, Zoltan Istvan

> From the novel *The Transhumanist Wager*:
>
> MATHEMATICAL FACT: The amount of life hours the United States Government is stealing from its citizens is a million times more than all the American life hours lost in the Twin Towers tragedy, the AIDS epidemic, and World War II combined. Demand that your government federally fund transhuman research, nullify anti-science laws, and promote a life extension culture. The average human body can be made to live healthily and productively beyond age 150.

****

57) A Bond with Hungary

In 1968, before I was born, my parents illegally escaped Communist-occupied Hungary. A few years before that, my uncle—a Hungarian freedom fighter—also left Hungary. He was wanted by Communist authorities. I sometimes think my blood line's revolutionary spirit has carried over to me. Perhaps it's a genetic trait. Because now I'm running for the US Presidency in 2016, and my core message is that if you vote for me, I will grant American citizens much longer lifespans through the use of radical science and technology. In fact, as President, I would use government funding to conquer human mortality altogether.

To some people, that is as radical thinking as one can get.

But let me back up. I was born in Los Angeles, California in 1973. In my 20s, I received my Hungarian passport, because as a working journalist for *National Geographic,* it was safer to travel under a Hungarian passport than an American one. I was assigned to a number of stories that involved conflict zones, including the Kashmir War between India and Pakistan. I also did a lot of traveling in the Middle East.

Later in my 30s, I had a life changing incident with a close call with a land mine while on a journalist assignment. It made me give up my dangerous journalist lifestyle, and dedicate my energy to the field of transhumanism--an international social movement that aims to use science and technology to improve the human being. The main goal of transhumanism is overcoming death using science and technology. It's a strange goal, but in the 21st Century it's increasingly possible. Already studies have been done that can stop and reverse aging in mice, and robotic hearts and stem cells have enabled human life to be much, much longer. Soon, in maybe 25 years, we may be able to engineer aging out of the human species altogether. In fact, I'm basing my US Presidential campaign on this idea—that if America put one trillion dollars toward life extension science, in just one decade we would be able to overcome human mortality.

Some people are afraid of technology and science and when it is so transformative to the species. But I think people will get used to it, just like they got used to cell phones, jet airplanes, and the internet. When I was 21 years old, I left for a sail trip around the world on my seven-meter yacht *The Way*. I was afraid and not sure I would survive the trip. But years later—after visiting about 70 countries via the boat—I was thrilled I made the choice to sail the oceans. Few experiences in my life have given me so much freedom, life, and time to just get to know myself.

Adventure and being free-spirited, no matter what you do, is critical to every person who wants to discover their best inner self. I've often believed it should be a law that everyone must travel abroad to at least 10 countries and three continents in their lifetime. This way, they experience new culture and new ways to see the world. It gives us a healthy respect for other cultures and introduces us to brand new ideas.

For me, Hungary is one of the places I have traveled many times and always enjoy. I still have many relatives in Hungary, but sadly, some have died now from old age. Many of my relatives have also now come to America, following the rest of my family. While I don't speak much Hungarian, I understand it almost fluently, since I grew up often hearing it in my household.

I share a strong bond with Hungary. For such a small country, I am constantly amazed at how many strong, newsworthy individuals it has produced over the centuries. Perhaps I will add to that special list by doing well in the US Presidency in 2016. If not, I hope I hope I will at least bring attention to the field of transhumanism, which aims to make everyone live longer, healthier, and better.

****

58) Feature Documentary *IMMORTALITY OR BUST* Press Release

Feature Documentary "Immortality or Bust" on Zoltan Istvan and the Transhumanism Movement Wins Breakout Award at Upcoming Raw Science Film Festival in Los Angeles

A feature documentary on US Presidential candidate Zoltan Istvan and his Immortality Bus will have its international debut this Saturday, June 26 2019, at the Raw Science Film Festival in Los Angeles at the historic United Artist Theatre. Featuring dozens of high profile journalists and scientists, the film explores the emerging landscape of the life extension, biohacking, and transhumanism movements.

The documentary covers a 38-foot coffin-shaped bus The New York Times Magazine called "the great brown sarcophagus of the American highway…a metaphor of life itself."

LOS ANGELES (PRWEB) JANUARY 25, 2019

Controversial feature documentary *Immortality or Bust* wins the Breakout Award at the upcoming Raw Science Film Festival in Los Angeles. The documentary covers a 38-foot coffin-shaped bus The New York Times Magazine called "the great brown sarcophagus of the American highway…a metaphor of life itself." The Immortality Bus has become one the most widely recognized and contentious activist projects in the transhumanist movement, after it gained over 100 million views during Zoltan Istvan's 2016 US Presidential campaign. Transhumanism's primary goal is to overcome biological death with science and technology.

Journalist Dylan Matthews of *Vox*, embedded on the bus, wrote, "Zoltan's obsessions are weird, but so was Al Gore's fascination with climate change in the 80s." In an 11,000 word feature about the bus, *The Verge* wrote Zoltan is like "some modern-day Ken Kesey."

The 77-min documentary features Zoltan's involvement into futurist politics, science activism, the transhumanist community, and his complex marriage and family life in San Francisco. Zoltan's medical doctor wife and her skepticism are a highlight in the film. The documentary also shows Zoltan's father, Steven Gyurko, and his untimely death, which occurred soon after he voted for his son for US President. Exclusive personal footage of the body and Zoltan's last words to his dad are emotionally shown.

Many significant science figures and journalists are in the documentary, and not always supportive of Zoltan's political quest. Some notable figures Zoltan meets include Libertarian Gary Johnson, cryptocurrency expert John McAfee, futurist Jacque Fresco, and comedian Jimmy Dore. Conspiracy theorist Alex Jones also briefly shows up and bashes Zoltan. Also covered is Zoltan's interview with Anonymous—the only known presidential candidate to have interviewed with the massive underground collective.

Filmed intensely over three years and already on the radar of Netflix, HBO, and Amazon Prime, director and film veteran Daniel Sollinger has high hopes this documentary will be widely viewed. The film's international debut is this Saturday, January 26, 2019 at 2:11PM at the historic 1700-seat United Artists Theatre at the ACE Hotel, 929 S Broadway, Los Angeles, California. The 5th Annual Raw Science Film Festival is timed to compete directly against Sundance Film Festival in order to provide a science-focused alternative to filmgoers.

Istvan, Sollinger, and others in *Immortality of Bust* will be at the black-tie optional award ceremony to receive their prize and give speeches. A press line on the red carpet starts at 5PM, followed by awards and an after party.

For more information or a private screening, contact Daniel Sollinger at:
Daniel Sollinger / Immortality or Bust
ds@danielsollinger.com
818-613-6044

Zoltan Istvan is also available for more information and interviews:
info@zoltanistvan.com
415-802-4891
http://www.zoltanistvan.com
@zoltan_istvan

****

59) Foreword for Chris T. Armstrong's Book *At Any Cost: A Guide to the Transhumanist Wager and the Ideas of Zoltan Istvan*

When I wrote *The Transhumanist Wager*, I hoped it might one day have an active life of its own. Seven years after publishing it, it seems to have found that life. Between inquiries from major Hollywood studios about optioning it, to philosophy professors regularly teaching it in their classes, to strangers on the street asking me for autographs, the novel has grown to be an essential vision of the transhumanist movement.

Of course, I'm thrilled with that, as I am with Chris T. Armstrong's new book *At Any Cost: A Guide to The Transhumanist Wager and the Ideas of Zoltan Istvan.* When Chris approached me a few years ago to write the definitive guide book to *The Transhumanist Wager*, I told him I'd help him in any way I could.

Over the years, sometimes well past midnight, I would get emails from Chris asking a peculiar question about Jethro

Knights, or why I chose the name the floating utopia in the novel Transhumania, or if the character Reverend Bolinas represented someone particular in real life. Chris explored thousands of minute details in the way a passionate detective might, sometimes even forcing me to examine what I really meant in the book, or if there could be multiple meanings.

An artist cannot work in a vacuum. I wrote *The Transhumanist Wager* in hopes to inspire others to engage in the quest to overcome death with science and technology; accomplishing this is a team effort for all of humanity. I also wrote it because it was time for a literary work that wasn't afraid to be a technological manifesto dedicated to upgrading the human being into something far better than it was. Chris has taken on that challenge, and is making his own transhumanist wager with this guide book.

It is therefore with great pleasure that I write the foreword here, and introduce *At Any Cost*. May you find something precious in the transhumanism movement and this book that appeals to your inner desire to become far more than you are now. May you—like Jethro Knights—live as long as you wish.

Zoltan Istvan / September 29, 2020

****

For more information or a private screening, contact Daniel Sollinger at:
Daniel Sollinger / Immortality or Bust
ds@danielsollinger.com
818-613-6044

Zoltan Istvan is also available for more information and interviews:
info@zoltanistvan.com
415-802-4891
http://www.zoltanistvan.com
@zoltan_istvan

****

59) Foreword for Chris T. Armstrong's Book *At Any Cost: A Guide to the Transhumanist Wager and the Ideas of Zoltan Istvan*

When I wrote *The Transhumanist Wager*, I hoped it might one day have an active life of its own. Seven years after publishing it, it seems to have found that life. Between inquiries from major Hollywood studios about optioning it, to philosophy professors regularly teaching it in their classes, to strangers on the street asking me for autographs, the novel has grown to be an essential vision of the transhumanist movement.

Of course, I'm thrilled with that, as I am with Chris T. Armstrong's new book *At Any Cost: A Guide to The Transhumanist Wager and the Ideas of Zoltan Istvan.* When Chris approached me a few years ago to write the definitive guide book to *The Transhumanist Wager*, I told him I'd help him in any way I could.

Over the years, sometimes well past midnight, I would get emails from Chris asking a peculiar question about Jethro

Knights, or why I chose the name the floating utopia in the novel Transhumania, or if the character Reverend Bolinas represented someone particular in real life. Chris explored thousands of minute details in the way a passionate detective might, sometimes even forcing me to examine what I really meant in the book, or if there could be multiple meanings.

An artist cannot work in a vacuum. I wrote *The Transhumanist Wager* in hopes to inspire others to engage in the quest to overcome death with science and technology; accomplishing this is a team effort for all of humanity. I also wrote it because it was time for a literary work that wasn't afraid to be a technological manifesto dedicated to upgrading the human being into something far better than it was. Chris has taken on that challenge, and is making his own transhumanist wager with this guide book.

It is therefore with great pleasure that I write the foreword here, and introduce *At Any Cost*. May you find something precious in the transhumanism movement and this book that appeals to your inner desire to become far more than you are now. May you—like Jethro Knights—live as long as you wish.

Zoltan Istvan / September 29, 2020

****

CHAPTER VII: COMMISSIONED XPRIZE SCREENPLAY

60) XPRIZE Longevity Animated Screenplay: Humanity's Greatest Quest

Title: *Humanity's Greatest Quest*

ACT I

(Scene: A group of 25 people in a sprawling cemetery surround a coffin about to be lowered into a grave. Dark clouds linger above the landscape but there is sun in the far distance. The people around the grave are all different genders, ethnicities, and age. Some are well dressed, some are not. One man is in a wheelchair. One older woman has a walker. A frocked pastor is presiding over the funeral. One young woman is holding a sleeping infant.)

Abruptly, one 75-year-old man named George turns to a young Asian woman, Lam, and asks:

"Do you know what the greatest humanitarian quest in the world is?"

Lam looks at him with surprise, but answers: *"No, I don't."*

George: *"Here's a hint: If successful, it will save one billion lives in just a 20-year period."*

Lam looks off into the distant at all the tombstones in the cemetery. She is skeptical, asking, *"One billion lives?'*

(Video briefly shows endless tombstones)

George: *"Here's another hint: It's a quest that will save more lives than all the deaths in all the wars in human history combined."*

(Video shows brief animated images of war and fighting)

George continues: *"Nothing as ambitious in human history like this has ever been attempted. Everyone from Nobel prize winners to billionaires to Hollywood stars to Heads of State have joined the quest. Even companies like Google have joined it."*

Lam looks astonished. So does Linda, an African American middle-aged woman standing behind George who has been listening to him. Linda leans over and asks: *"What is it? What's this quest?"*

George: *"Stopping human death through science."*

The pastor looks sternly at George, Lam, and Linda. Then the pastor begins addressing the mourners. But the Pastor's voice quickly drifts off into the distance and the scene focuses back on George.

ACT II

(New visual perspective of funeral from different angle, showing sun coming closer to cemetery.)

An Indian man named Rashish, to the right of George asks: *"But what will a future without death look like?"*

George looks at Rashish and says: *"Let me show you."*

(Scene changes entirely. Point of view perspective of viewers see into the future, drifting magically in the air looking down at people and modern busy towns. Scene shows some radial new technologies, like self-flying drone taxis, action sports requiring exoskeleton suits, immersive virtual reality holograms, etc. The future looks fun and inviting.

George narrates to the group traveling to the future with him: *"The future will be amazing. But there's still a terrible problem."*

George points down and says: *Take a look: The greatest tragedy we all know is not having enough time alive."*

(Video shows scene of busy life, of workers working endlessly, of marriage, of having babies, but also of aging through it all, and finally, of never having enough time to accomplishing one's greatest goals and most heartfelt desires. This video montage of life, despite the amazing advances, is depressing and overwhelming.)

George: *"But in a deathless future, you'll always have enough time. You can do five PhDs. And then still join a rock band and play lead guitar. And then you can still learn to surf and move to Hawaii. And you can finally read all the classics on your bookshelf."*

(Video shows accompanying images to George's words).

Lam breaks in: *"But what about aging? I don't want to live forever as a super old person who's too weak to get out of bed."*

(Video shows challenges of extreme old age)

George: *"Don't worry, the key to overcoming human death is defeating aging. In the future, science could stop and even reverse aging. New medicines and technology will rejuvenate your body to the age you want. Scientists will do it with stem cells and 3D printed body parts. They'll give you bionic organs—like a perfect heart--that are better than your natural ones. Or they might just genetically enhance when you're young not to age past 40 and to never get disease. Scientists are working on all this technology right now."*

(Video shows all these different technologies via scientists in laboratories)

Linda asks: *"Are these scientists having success?"*

George: *"Yes, lots of it. In the last few years, billions of dollars have flowed into the life extension and transhumanist research. A cultural shift around the world is happening and people are becoming open to this type of radical change. In fact, some technologists think we'll even be able to upload our consciousness into a computer someday as a way of immortality."*

(Video shows brain to machine interface and investors pouring in money to the life extension technologies)

George continues: *"Lately, with so many great scientists working on different ways of overcoming aging and medical trauma, death is no longer what it once was. Death was once accepted as natural, unavoidable fate. But today, the human body is understood more as a complex machine—and machines can be tampered with, modified, remade, and most importantly, improved. Any future is possible if we put in enough effort to change our bodies and the world."*

(Video shows scene of scientists fixing body in radical ways, like 3D printing hearts, and of people coming back from dead on operating table due to medical advances).

ACT III (final act):

(Video scene goes back to original scene of funeral. Sun is almost shining now, breaking through the clouds.)

The man in the wheelchair rolls in towards the group, and asks: *"But how long will it take to get to this future?"*

George answers: *"It depends on you."*

George points to Lam, Linda, and Rashish, and says: *"And it also depends on you, you, and you. It depends on all of us."*

(Video shows different facial expressions of people in the group).

George continues: *"Experts think if we put enough resources into this moon shot, we could achieve it in just a decade or two—hopefully by 2040. But we have to dedicate our time, energy, and resources today. There's not a moment to lose."*

George: "Each one of us is dying right now. Our cells are aging and losing the battle against death. We are all born terminal. The fight to stay alive indefinitely is now--right now!"

George looks sadly at the casket, saying quietly: *"Unfortunately, it's too late to help those who have already lost their lives."*

(New video scene of pastor walking over to George. Paster gently touches George's shoulder)

The Pastor says: *"George, it's time to say good-bye to you wife."*

George looks at the group and says. *"We were married 50 years—far too short for the love of my life. Modern medicine couldn't keep her alive. But in the near future, it can keep all of you alive if you dedicate yourself to this quest and help improve humanity's odds. We're all in this together. Every moment counts to get to a future where death no longer devastates our lives and takes away those that we love most."*

(Video scene of George putting a rose on the casket. Casket begins to lower into the ground. Image fades out).

****

APPENDIX

1) A version of *A Chip in my Hand Unlocks my House. Why Does that Scare People?* first appeared in *The New York Times*

2) A version of *The New Bionic Sports of the Future Transhumanist Olympics* first appeared in *Vice*

3) A version of *#TalktoMe: Futurist Zoltan Istvan Interviews his Aging Father* first appeared in *HuffPost*

4) A version of *Cybernetics: More Transhuman than Human; Rumination on Cybernetic Technology* first appeared in *Flaunt*

5) A version of *A TEDx Talk Celebrating Scientists and Exploring the Technological Future of Beauty* first appeared in *HuffPost*

6) A version of *Will Brain Wave Technology Eliminate the Need for a Second Language?* first appeared in *HuffPost*

7) A version of *Quartz: We Asked Some of the Boldest Thinkers What the World will be like in 50 Years. Here's what Zoltan Istvan Told Us* first appeared in *Quartz*

8) A version of *The 5 Most Revolutionary Scientific Trends to Look Out For (2017)* first appeared in *Vice*

9) A version of *The First International Beauty Contest Judged by Robots* first appeared in *TechCrunch*

10) A version of *Major Transhumanism Conference Features Both Rising and Seasoned Experts* first appeared in *HuffPost*

11) *Is College Worth It? What Would You Have Paid to Get Your Degree?* was first published in this book

12) A version of *The Augmented Expo in San Jose was Fascinating* was first published in *HuffPost*

13) A version of *Think Driverless Cars Will be Modern-looking and Reduce Traffic. Think Again* was first published in *Vice*

14) A version of *I Tried Direct Neurofeedback and the Results Surprised Me* was first published in *Psychology Today*

15) A version of *A Transhumanist Goes to the Presidential Conventions* was first published in *Vice*

16) A version of *The Libertarian Futurist's Case for Avoiding War and Military Entanglements* was first published in *HuffPost*

17) A version of *Is Monetizing Federal Land the Way to Pay for Basic Income?* was first published in *TechCrunch*

18) A version of *Why I'm Not Taking Any Contributions for my Presidential Run* was first published in *Business Insider*

19) A version of *To Grow 3rd Party Politics in America, Make John McAfee the Libertarian Party Nominee (Updated Version)* was first published in *HuffPost*

20) A version of *Gary Johnson Wants Driverless Secret Service Cars and a US-Led Gene Editing Revolution* was first published in *Futurism*

21) *I Went to the Largest Freedom Festival in the World and Here's What I Saw* was first published in this book

22) A version of *Another Wild Week in my Transhumanism Campaign* was first published in *HuffPost*

23) A version of *I Want My Felonies Back* was first published in *Reason*

24) Quotes from *Should We Also Have A Small Private Market for the Coronavirus Vaccine?* was first published in *The Washington Times (*by Jennifer Harper), then the full essay was published in this book

25) A version of *Wanted: A New Psychology; Interview with Futurist Gray Scott* was first published in *Psychology Today*

26) A version of *Transhumanist Nikola Danaylov Faces Tragedy with Resolve* was first published in *Psychology Today*

27) A version of *Gennady Stolyarov: A Children's Book Ponders Death* was first published in *Psychology Today*

28) A version of *Interview with Transhumanism Advocate Riva-Melissa Tez* was first published in *Psychology Today*

29) A version of *Interview with Transhumanist Activist Hank Pellissier* was first published in *Psychology Today*

30) A version of *Exploring a New Type of Community: Zero State* was first published in *Psychology Today*

31) A version of Women in STEM, Transhumanism, and a New Author to Watch was first published in *Psychology Today*

32) A version of *TransEvolution, Transhumanism, and Daniel Estulin* was first published in *Psychology Today*

33) A version of *Interview with Transhumanist Biohacker Rich Lee* was first published in *Psychology Today*

34) A version of *Author David Simpson Talks Transhumanism in Science Fiction* was first published in *Psychology Today*

35) A version of *Longevity Cookbook is Your Chance to Defeat Aging: Interview with Maria Konovalenko* was first published in *Psychology Today*

36) A version of *Dr. Bertalan Mesko: A Medical Futurist Discusses Health and Transhumanism* was first published in *Psychology Today*

37) A version *Discovering a Bush Tribe in the South Pacific* was first published on *NationalGeographic.com*

38) A version of *Does Landmark Unmanned Flight Spell Doom for Test
Pilots?* was first published on *NationalGeographic.com*

39) A version of *For the Athens 2004 Olympic Games, Environmental Stakes are High* was first published via *The New York Times Syndicate*

40) A version of *The World Under Sail* first appeared in *Good Old Boat* magazine

41) A version of *Travel! Intrigue! Cannibals! Extreme Journalism at Far Ends of Earth* first appeared in *The San Francisco Chronicle*

42) A version of *Becoming a Treasure Hunter* first appeared in *International Living*

43) A version of *The X Factor: My Pirate Attack off Yemen* first appeared in *Clamor Magazine*

44) A version of *Greening the Iron Curtain* first appeared in *Outside* magazine

45) A version of *The Mondavi of Pot* first appeared in *The Daily Caller*

46) A version of *Sad News: My Dad Steven Gyurko has Died* first appeared in Zoltan Istvan's social media

47) *A Twitter Conversation Between Harvard University Center for Bioethics Faculty Member Dr. Louise Perkins King and Transhumanist Zoltan Istvan* first appeared on Twitter

48) A version of *I Almost Died from a Leading American Killer: Choking on Food* first appeared in *Marin Independent Journal*

49) A version of *Interview with my Mom, Ilona Gyurko* first appeared on Zoltan Istvan's YouTube channel

50) A version of *Quotes and Reactions from my Wife, Dr. Lisa Memmel* first appeared in documentary *Immortality or Bust*

51) Poem: *Death* first appeared in this book

52) Song: *The Anti-You* first appeared in this book

53) A version of *Cato Institute's Cato Unbound Debate: A Rebuttal: Deniers and Critics of AI Will Only Be Left Behind* first appeared in *Cato Unbound*

54) *Remarks on my Novel The Transhumanist Wager* first appeared in this book

55) *Stop Impersonating me on Senior Dating Sites, Donating Fake Twitter Followers to My Presidential Campaign, and Vandalizing my Wikipedia Page* first appeared in this book

56) *On Culture's Humanicide* first appeared in this book

57) A version of *A Bond with Hungary* was commissioned by *Elle*. First publication is unknown

58) *Feature Documentary IMMORTALITY OR BUST Press Release* was first released on *PRNewswire.com*

59) *Foreword for Chris T. Armstrong's Book At Any Cost: A Guide to the Transhumanist Wager and the Ideas of Zoltan Istvan* first appeared in Mr. Armstrong's book

60) *XPRIZE Longevity Screenplay: Humanity's Greatest Quest* first appeared on XPRIZE's website

****

AUTHOR'S BIOGRAPHY

With his popular 2016 US Presidential run as a science candidate, bestselling book *The Transhumanist Wager*, and influential speeches at institutions like the World Bank and World Economic Forum, Zoltan Istvan has spearheaded the transformation of transhumanism into a thriving worldwide phenomenon. He is often cited as a global leader of the radical science movement. Formerly a journalist for National Geographic, Zoltan frequently writes for major media, appears on television, and also consults for organizations like the US Navy, XPRIZE, and government of Dubai. His futurist work, speeches, and promotion of radical science have reached hundreds of millions of people. Award-winning feature documentary *IMMORTALITY OR BUST* on his work is now on Amazon Prime. A recent project is his 7-book box set of writings and essays titled the *Zoltan Istvan Futurist Collection*, a #1 bestseller in Essays on Amazon. Zoltan studied Philosophy at Columbia University and the University of Oxford, and now lives in San Francisco with his physician wife and two daughters. Visit his website at: www.zoltanistvan.com

****

ABOUT THE BOOK

After publishing his bestselling novel *The Transhumanist Wager* in 2013, Zoltan Istvan began frequently writing essays about the future. A former journalist with National Geographic, Istvan's essays spanned topics from the Singularity to cyborgism to radical longevity to futurist philosophy. He also wrote about politics as he made a surprisingly popular run for the US Presidency in 2016, touring the country aboard his coffin-shaped Immortality Bus, which *The New York Times Magazine* called "The great sarcophagus of the American highway…a metaphor of life itself." Zoltan's provocative campaign and radical tech-themed articles garnered him the title of the "Science Candidate" by his supporters. Many of his writings—published in *Vice, Quartz, Slate, The Guardian, International Living, Yahoo! News, Gizmodo, TechCruch, Psychology Today, Salon, New Scientist, Business Insider, The Daily Dot, Maven, Cato Institute, The Daily Caller, Metro, International Business Times, Wired UK, IEEE Spectrum, The San Francisco Chronicle, Newsweek,* and *The New York Times*—went viral on the internet, garnishing millions of reads and tens of thousands of comments. His articles—often seen as controversial, provocative, and secular—elevated him to worldwide recognition as one of the de facto leaders of the burgeoning transhumanism movement. Here are many of those watershed essays again, organized, edited, and occasionally readapted by the author in this comprehensive nonfiction work, *The Remnants: Essays, Interviews, and Other Writings.* Also included are some of Zoltan's new writings, never published before. This book is part of a 7-book box set collection of his essential work, the *Zoltan Istvan Futurist Collection*, focusing on futurism, secularism, life extension, politics, philosophy, transhumanism and his early writings. He partially edited the collection during his studies at the University of Oxford. Enjoy reading about the future according to Zoltan Istvan.

www.ingramcontent.com/pod-product-compliance
Lightning Source LLC
LaVergne TN
LVHW051552070426
835507LV00021B/2542